The Updated Ninja Foodi
Recipe Book for UK

Embark on a 2000-Day Culinary Discovery Journey with the Ninja Cookbook for Beginners

to Master the Kitchen and Gain Expertise in Making Homemade Cuisine

Billy Morley

CONTENTS

Introduction

The Ninja Foodi Max Multi-Cooker is a versatile appliance that can be used for a variety of cooking methods. It is a great addition to any kitchen. The cooker comes with a reversible rack, so you can steam vegetables or seafood. It also has a slow cooker function, so you can make soups or stews. The Ninja MAX Multi-Cooker is also very easy to clean, which is a huge bonus. It can be used as a pressure cooker, slow cooker, air fryer, steamer, and more. The Ninja Foodi Max Multi-Cooker comes with a 6.5-quart ceramic-coated pot and a 5-quart cook and crisp basket. It also includes a steaming rack, a Ninja Foodi recipe book, and a quick start guide. This book is packed with delicious recipes that are perfect for the Ninja Foodi Max Multi-Cooker. From breakfast to dinner, and everything in between, you'll find something to love in this cookbook. The Ninja Foodi Max Multi-Cooker is a versatile appliance that can do it all. It can be used as a slow cooker, a pressure cooker, or an air fryer. It also has a steamer function. The Ninja Foodi Max Multi-Cooker is a great appliance for those who want to have a versatile cooker in their kitchen. With this cookbook, you'll learn how to use your Ninja Foodi Max Multi-Cooker to its full potential. You will also get to know the fundamentals and maintenance of this amazing kitchen appliance. You'll be whipping up delicious meals in no time!

Important Safeguards

The Ninja Max Multi-Cooker is the perfect appliance for those who love to cook. It is a multi-cooker that can be used to cook rice, pasta, chicken, beef, and vegetables. The Ninja Max Multi-Cooker is also perfect for those who want to make soup, stew, or chili. The Ninja Max Multi-Cooker is also great for making a pot of coffee or tea. The Ninja Max Multi-Cooker is easy to use and comes with a user manual. The Ninja Max Multi-Cooker is also dishwasher safe. When you're cooking, it's important to take some basic safety precautions to ensure that your food is cooked properly and doesn't pose a risk to your health. Here are some important safeguards to follow when using your Ninja Max Multi-Cooker:
• Read the instruction manual carefully before use.
• Do not use the cooker if it is damaged or malfunctioning.
• Keep the cooker clean, both inside and out.
• Do not use the Ninja Max Multi-Cooker if the power cord is damaged.
• Keep the Ninja Max Multi-Cooker away from children and pets.
• Do not place the Ninja Max Multi-Cooker on or near hot surfaces.
• Do not place the Ninja Max Multi-Cooker in a wet area.
• Do not use the Ninja Max Multi-Cooker if it is leaking.
• Do not use the Ninja Max Multi-Cooker if the pot is not properly seated on the base

Parts and Accessories

The unit comes with a variety of accessories that can be used to help you create delicious meals. If you're looking for a versatile and convenient way to cook, the Ninja Max Multi-Cooker is a great option. This all-in-one appliance can be used as a slow cooker, pressure cooker, and steamer, making it a versatile addition to your kitchen. The Ninja Max Multi-Cooker also features a browning function, so you can brown meat or vegetables before cooking them. With so many functions, the Ninja Max Multi-Cooker is a versatile and convenient addition to your kitchen. The Ninja Max Multi-Cooker comes with a steaming basket that can be used to

cook seafood, veggies, and more. The unit also comes with a frying basket that can be used to fry chicken, fish, and more. With these accessories, the Ninja Max Multi-Cooker can be used for a variety of cooking tasks. This makes it a versatile kitchen appliance that can be used for many different recipes.

Using Control Panel

Function Buttons

PRESSURE: Use to cook food quickly while maintaining tenderness.
STEAM: Use to gently cook delicate foods at a high temperature.
SLOW COOK: Cook your food at a lower temperature for longer periods of time.
YOGURT: Pasteurise and ferment milk for creamy homemade yogurt.
SEAR/SAUTÉ: To use the unit as a stovetop for browning meats, sautéing vegetables, simmering sauces and more.
AIR CRISP: Give foods crispiness and crunch with little to no oil.
BAKE/ROAST: Use the unit like an oven for tender meats, baked treats and more.
GRILL: Use high temperature to caramelise and brown your food.
DEHYDRATE: Dehydrate meats, fruits and vegetables for healthy snacks.
KEEP WARM: After pressure cooking, steaming, or slow cooking, the unit will automatically switch to Keep Warm mode and start counting up. Keep Warm will stay on for 12 hours, or you may press KEEP WARM to turn it off. Keep Warm mode is not intended to warm food from a cold state but to keep it warm at a food-safe temperature.

Operation Buttons

The appliance has a number of buttons that can be used to select the desired cooking function. The following is a brief overview of the function buttons on the Ninja Max Multi-Cooker. The POWER button is used to turn the appliance on and off. The "TIME" button is used to set the cooking time. The "TEMP" button is used to set the cooking temperature. The "FUNCTION" button is used to select the desired cooking function. The START/STOP button is used to start and stop the cooking cycle.

Before First Use

If you've never used a Ninja Max Multi-Cooker before, there are a few things you should know before you get started. Here's what you need to know to get the most out of your new appliance. Read the manual. Yes, we know it's boring, but it's important. The manual will tell you everything you need to know about your new Ninja Max, from how to use all the features to troubleshooting tips. Clean it before you use it. Even if it's brand new, you should always clean your Ninja Max before you use it. Just run it through a cycle with some soapy water and it'll be good to go. Don't overfill it. The Ninja Max has a max fill line for a reason. Don't go over that line or you risk damaging your appliance. Be careful with the blades. The blades on the Ninja Max are super sharp, so be careful when handling them.

Install the Condensation Collector

One of the most popular items in the kitchen these days is the Ninja MAX Multi-Cooker. This handy little appliance can do it all, from cooking rice and steaming vegetables, to slow cooking meats and even baking cakes. And one of the best things about the Ninja MAX Multi-Cooker is that it comes with a built-in condensation collector.

What is a condensation collector?

A condensation collector is a small device that sits on top of the Ninja MAX Multi-Cooker and collects any condensation that forms during the cooking process. This condensation is then funneled back into the Ninja MAX Multi-Cooker, where it can be used to help cook the food.

Why is a condensation collector important?

A condensation collector is important because it helps to keep the Ninja MAX Multi-Cooker clean and free of water spots. It also helps to prevent any water from getting into the food, which can ruin the taste.

How to install condensation collector?

If you've ever used a Ninja MAX Multi-Cooker, you know that it's a powerhouse when it comes to cooking. But one thing it's not so great at is collecting condensation. That's why we've put together this quick guide on how to install the Ninja MAX Multi-Cooker Condensation Collector. The Condensation Collector is a must-have accessory if you want to get the most out of your Ninja MAX Multi-Cooker. It's designed to collect any condensation that might otherwise drip down into the cooking pot, keeping your food nice and dry. Installing the Condensation Collector is a breeze. Simply remove the pot from the Ninja MAX Multi-Cooker and set it aside.

Then, take the Condensation Collector and place it over the top of the opening where the pot goes.

Removing and Reinstalling the Anti-Clog Cap

If you love your Ninja Multi-Cooker but are tired of dealing with clogged vents, then you need the Anti-Clog Cap Ninja MAX Multi-Cooker! This nifty little accessory fits right onto your Ninja Multi-Cooker and prevents clogs by keeping food particles from getting into the vent. It's easy to use and clean, and it's a must-have for any Ninja Multi-Cooker owner. If your Ninja MAX Multi-Cooker is starting to experience clogging issues, don't worry - this is easily fixable! All you need to do is remove the anti-clog cap and give it a good cleaning. Here's how:
• Unplug your Ninja MAX Multi-Cooker from the wall outlet.
• Remove the pot and lid from the base.
• Locate the anti-clog cap on the underside of the lid.
• Use a Phillips head screwdriver to remove the two screws that secure the cap in place.
• Carefully remove the cap, being careful not to lose the small O-ring that sits on top of the cap.
• Rinse the cap and O-ring in warm, soapy water.
• Use a soft-bristled brush to clean any debris from the small holes in the cap.
If your Ninja MAX Multi-Cooker is not functioning properly, one troubleshooting step you can take is to reinstall the Anti-Clog Cap. This cap is located on the underside of the lid and helps to prevent food particles from clogging the pressure cooker's valve. To reinstall the cap, simply unscrew the old one and screw on a new one in its place. Be sure to hand-tighten the new cap until it is snug. Here's how to do it:
• Unplug the Ninja MAX from the power outlet.
• Remove the pot from the Ninja MAX.
• Locate the Anti-Clog Cap on the underside of the Ninja MAX lid.
• Unscrew the Anti-Clog Cap from the lid.
• Screw on a new one in its place

Benefits of Using It

When it comes to mealtime, the Ninja MAX Multi-Cooker is a true powerhouse. This versatile appliance can do it all, from slow cooking and steaming to frying and baking. And with so many features and functions, it's no wonder the Ninja MAX Multi-Cooker is a favorite among home cooks. This unique appliance offers all the benefits of a slow cooker, pressure cooker, and steamer all in one. Here are some benefits of using the Ninja MAX Multi-Cooker. It is one-pot cooking, with the Ninja MAX Multi-Cooker, you can cook an entire meal in one pot. This means less time spent cooking and more time enjoying your meal. The Ninja MAX Multi-Cooker is a versatile appliance that can be used for a variety of cooking methods. Whether

you want to slow cook, steam, fry, or bake, the Ninja MAX Multi-Cooker can do it all. It is perfect for large families. The Ninja MAX Multi-Cooker can cook enough food for up to 8 people at once. If you have a large family, the Ninja MAX Multi-Cooker is perfect. It's a time saver. With the Ninja MAX Multi-Cooker, you can cook an entire meal in one pot. This means less time spent cooking and cleaning up. The Ninja MAX Multi-Cooker can be used to cook a wide variety of foods. It's easy to use. The Ninja MAX Multi-Cooker is very user-friendly and comes with an easy-to-follow instruction manual.

Step-by-Step Using Ninja Foodi MAX Multi-Cooker

If you're looking for a versatile cooker that can do it all, the Ninja Foodi MAX Multi-Cooker is a perfect choice. This all-in-one appliance can pressure cook, air fry, steam, slow cook, sear/sauté, and bake – all in one pot. And with a 6.5-quart capacity, it's big enough to cook for the whole family. First, let's start with the basics. The Ninja Foodi MAX Multi-Cooker has a 6.5-quart capacity, making it perfect for cooking large meals. It also has a 1400-watt heating element, which means it can reach high temperatures quickly. The Ninja Foodi MAX also has an air fryer basket, a steam rack, and a reversible cooking plate. Before you get started, make sure to read the manual that comes with your Ninja Foodi MAX. This will help you understand how the appliance works and what safety precautions you need to take. Here's a step-by-step guide to using your Ninja Foodi MAX Multi-Cooker:

Select Your Desired Cooking Function/Mode: The options are pressure cooking, slow cooking, steaming, searing/sautéing, baking, broiling, and air frying. You can choose depending on what you're looking to cook.

Select Your Cooking Time: Depending on the cooking function you've chosen, you'll need to set the timer for the desired cook time.

Add Your Ingredients: To get started, simply add your ingredients to the pot. There's no need to pre-cook anything – the Ninja Foodi MAX will do all the work for you.

Stove Top: Assuming you have all the ingredients you need, the first thing you'll want to do is gather everything together and prep your ingredients. This means chopping any vegetables you'll be using and measuring out any dry goods like rice or quinoa. Once everything is ready to go, you can plug in your Ninja MAX Multi-Cooker and select the "stove top" function.

Heat Up: Next, you'll want to add oil to the pot and let it heat up. Then, you can add in your chopped vegetables and cook them until they're soft. After that, you can add in your dry goods and any liquid you'll be using (like broth or water). Once everything is in the pot, simply put on the lid and let the Ninja MAX Multi-Cooker do its thing!

Remove the Lid: Depending on what you're making, the cooking time will vary. But once everything is cooked through, you can simply remove the lid and enjoy your delicious meal!

Swap to Top

In today's fast-paced world, we're always looking for ways to save time. That's why the Ninja Foodi MAX Multi-Cooker is such a great kitchen appliance. It not only cooks food quickly and easily but it can also be used to swap out ingredients. For example, let's say you're making a recipe that calls for diced tomatoes. But you only have whole tomatoes on hand. No problem! Just place the whole tomatoes in the Foodi MAX, and use the swap function to dice them. The same goes for any other ingredient you need to chop or dice. Not only does the Ninja Foodi MAX Multi-Cooker save you time in the kitchen, but it also makes meal prep a breeze. So if you're looking for a quick and easy way to get dinner on the table, this is the appliance for you.

Using the Crispy Lid

One of the best features of the Ninja MAX Multi-Cooker is the crispy lid. This allows you to cook food with a crispy, crunchy texture without using a lot of oil. Here are some tips on how to use the crispy lid:

• Preheat the lid by setting it to the "crisp" setting.
• Place your food on the cooking grate.
• Close the lid and cook for the recommended time.
• When the timer goes off, open the lid and check to see if your food is crispy. If

it's not, close the lid and cook for a few minutes longer.
• Once your food is crispy, remove it from the grill and enjoy!

Using the Cooking Functions with the Crispy Lid

Air Crisp

The Ninja MAX Multi-Cooker is a versatile appliance that can do it all, and one of its best features is the Air Crisp with Crispy Lid. This feature allows you to cook food with a crispy, crunchy texture without using any oil. Air Crisp is perfect for those who are looking to eat healthier, as it eliminates the need for unhealthy frying oils. And, since the Ninja MAX Multi-Cooker can also be used as an air fryer, you can cook up all of your favorite fried foods without any guilt. So, whether you're looking to make healthier versions of your favorite comfort foods or you're just trying to cut down on your oil consumption, the Air Crisp with Crispy Lid is a great option. Air Crisp with Crispy Lid in Ninja Multi-Cooker is a great way to cook food. The lid helps to keep the food moist and crispy. The lid also helps to brown the food. The lid is also dishwasher safe.

1. Preheat your Ninja Multi Cooker by selecting the Air Crisp function.
2. Place the food you wish to crisp on the air crisp tray.
3. Close the lid and cook according to your recipe.
4. Once done, open the lid and enjoy your crispy creation!

Grill

Grilling with a crispy lid is a great way to get that perfect sear on your food. But how do you do it? Here are some tips to help you get started.
• Preheat your grill to high heat.
• Place your food on the grill grates and close the lid.
• Cook for the recommended time, flipping once.
• Remove from grill and enjoy!

Bake/Roast

One of the best things about the Ninja Multi Cooker is its ability to bake with a crispy lid. This means that you can have perfectly cooked food with a crispy, golden brown top. Here are some tips on how to bake with a crispy lid:
• Preheat the Ninja Multi Cooker to the baking setting.
• Place the food that you want to bake in the cooking pot.
• Put the lid on the pot and make sure that it is locked in place.
• Set the timer for the desired cook time.
• When the timer goes off, open the lid and check the food. If it is not done, you can close the lid and cook for a few more minutes.
• Once the food is cooked, remove it from the pot and enjoy.

Dehydrate

Dehydrating with the lid on the Ninja Multi Cooker is a great way to preserve food. By removing the water content from foods, they can last for months or even years without spoiling. This process can be used for both fruits and vegetables and is a great way to have healthy snacks on hand that won't go bad. To dehydrate with the lid on the Ninja Multi Cooker, begin by washing and drying your fruits or vegetables. Cut them into thin slices, and then arrange them on the dehydrating racks that come with the cooker. Make sure that the slices are not touching, as this will prevent proper airflow and slow down the dehydrating process. Close the lid of the Ninja Multi Cooker, and select the "Dehydrate" function. Set the time for how long you want the dehydrating process to take, and then let the cooker do its job. Once the time is up, your fruits or vegetables will be dried and ready to store.

Get Started Pressure Cooking

Pressure cooking is a cooking method that uses high pressure and steam to cook food quickly. And with the Ninja Foodi Max, you can cook food up to 70% faster than traditional methods. Plus, the pressure cooking function has 11 settings so you can tailor it to your specific dish. One of the best things about pressure cooking is that it locks in flavor and nutrients. So, not only is your food cooked quickly but it's also packed full of flavor and goodness.

Installing and Removing the Pressure Lid

To use the pressure cooking function, the pressure lid must be installed. Here is a step-by-step guide on how to install the pressure lid:
• Make sure that the Ninja Max Multi Cooker is turned off and unplugged.

• Remove the lid by lifting it straight up.
• Take the pressure lid out of the box and remove any packaging materials.
• Place the pressure lid on top of the Ninja Max Multi Cooker, lining up the two tabs on the lid with the slots on the cooker.
• Press down on the lid until it clicks into place.

If you're like me, you love your Ninja MAX Multi Cooker. It's so versatile and convenient, and it's perfect for cooking large meals. But one thing that can be a pain is removing the pressure lid. Here's a quick and easy guide on how to do it:
• Start by making sure that the pressure release valve is in the "venting" position.
• Next, open the lid of the Ninja MAX Multi Cooker.
• You'll see two tabs on the underside of the pressure lid. Press down on these tabs and lift the lid off of the cooker.
• That's it! You've successfully removed the pressure lid.

Natural Pressure Release vs. Quick Pressure Release

There are a lot of different types of multi-cookers on the market these days. Some have more features than others, and some have specific functions that make them stand out from the crowd. So, which one is the best? The Ninja Max Multi-cooker is a great option for those who want a versatile and easy-to-use appliance. It has a 6-in-1 function that allows you to cook a variety of different foods, and it also has a quick-press release button that makes it easy to get your food out when it's done. If you're like most people, you probably don't think much about the pressure cooker sitting in your kitchen cupboard. But did you know that this humble kitchen appliance can be used for much more than just cooking food? A pressure cooker is a handy tool for natural pressure release. Simply put, the pressure cooker allows you to release pressure naturally, without having to rely on electricity or gas. This is perfect for those times when you're away from home and don't have access to these things. To use the pressure cooker for natural pressure release, simply place your food inside and seal the lid. Then, turn the pressure cooker on its side and wait for the pressure to release. This can take anywhere from a few minutes to an hour, depending on the amount of pressure that's been built up. Once the pressure has been released, you can then open the pressure cooker and remove your food. It's that easy! On the other hand, when you need to quickly release pressure from your Ninja Max Multi Cooker, use the quick-release valve. This will allow the steam to escape and the pressure to be released quickly. Be sure to use caution when doing this, as the steam can be hot.

Pressurizing

This process allows you to cook food faster and more evenly, giving you perfectly cooked meals every time. Here's a step-by-step guide to pressurizing your Ninja Foodi Max Multi-Cooker:
• Make sure that the cooker is turned off and that the pressure release valve is in the seal position.
• Add your food and liquid to the cooking pot, making sure not to

fill it more than halfway.
• Close the lid and turn the knob to the pressure cooking position.
• Press the pressure release valve to the vent position.
• Set the timer according to the recipe you're using.
• Once the timer goes off, turn the knob to the release position and wait for the pressure to release.

Using the Cooking Functions with the Pressure Lid

Pressure Cook

Pressure cookers have been around for centuries and they are a great way to cook food quickly and easily. There are many different types of pressure cookers on the market, but one of the best is the Ninja Foodi Max Multi Cooker. This pressure cooker is a great choice for anyone who wants an easy-to-use and convenient way to cook their food. The Ninja Foodi Max Multi Cooker is a great choice for anyone who wants an easy-to-use and convenient way to cook their food. This pressure cooker is a great choice for anyone who wants an easy-to-use and convenient way to cook their food. The Ninja Foodi Max Multi Cooker is a great choice for anyone who wants an easy-to-use and convenient way to cook their food. A pressure cooker is a kitchen appliance that cooks food by using high-pressure steam. This high-pressure steam helps to cook food faster than traditional methods. Additionally, the pressure cooker seals in nutrients, making it a healthy cooking option. The Ninja Max Multi Cooker is a great option for those looking for a pressure cooker. It is a 6-in-1 cooker that can pressure cook, slow cook, steam, sauté, and more. It also has a built-in Ninja Foodi® TenderCrisp™ Technology, which allows you to quickly cook and crisp food.

Steam

When it comes to cooking, few things are as important as having the right tools. This is especially true when it comes to choosing a pressure cooker. If you're looking for a top-of-the-line pressure cooker, the Ninja Max Multi Cooker is a great option. One of the most appealing features of the Ninja Max Multi Cooker is the fact that it has a steam pressure lid. This is a great feature for several reasons. First, it ensures that your food will be cooked evenly. Second, it allows you to cook multiple items at once. Third, it cuts down on cooking time. Another great feature of the Ninja Max Multi Cooker is the fact that it has a browning function. This is a great feature if you're looking to add a little bit of color to your food.

Slow Cook

You want to cook a tough cut of meat or stew until it is falling apart tender. The pressure lid also speeds up the cooking time, so it is perfect for those busy weeknights when you want a hearty meal but don't have all day to cook. Here are some tips for slow cooking with the pressure lid:
• Choose a tough cut of meat: Chuck roast, short ribs, or stew meat are all great choices.

- Season the meat generously with salt and pepper.
- Sear the meat in the Ninja Multi-Cooker before adding the liquid. This will help to create a rich, flavorful base for your stew.
- Add a small amount of liquid: Just enough to cover the bottom of the pot.
- Once the food is cooked, remove it from the pot and enjoy.

Yogurt

If you're looking for a delicious and healthy snack, yogurt is a great option. And if you want to make yogurt at home, the Ninja® Multi-Cooker can help. With the pressure lid, you can easily make yogurt in the Ninja® Multi-Cooker. Here's how:
- Add milk to the pot of the Ninja® Multi-Cooker.
- Place the pressure lid on the pot and select the "Yogurt" function.
- Set the time for 8 hours.
- After 8 hours, open the pressure lid and add your favorite yogurt starter.
- Close the pressure lid and select the "Yogurt" function again.
- Set the time for 2 hours.
- After 2 hours, open the pressure lid and transfer the yogurt to a container.
- Enjoy your homemade yogurt!

Sear/Saute

If you're looking for a Sear with a Pressure lid in a ninja multi-cooker, you've come to the right place. Here at Ninja®, we know that when it comes to cooking, every second counts. That's why we've designed our multi-cooker to not only be a powerful and versatile kitchen appliance but also to include a sear with a pressure lid. This unique feature allows you to sear meats and vegetables quickly and easily, without having to worry about the lid coming off and releasing all of the pressure. Plus, the sear with pressure lid also comes with a steamer basket, so you can cook multiple items at once. So whether you're looking to cook a delicious meal for your family or impress your guests at your next dinner party, the Sear with Pressure lid in ninja multi-cooker is a perfect choice.

Tips for Using Accessories

When it comes to small kitchen appliances, the Ninja Max Multi Cooker is one of the most versatile. With its ability to slow cook, steam, sauté, and more, this appliance can help you create a variety of healthy and delicious meals. To get the most out of your Ninja Max Multi Cooker, here are a few tips and tricks. Use the slow cook function to create hearty stews and soups. Simply add your ingredients to the pot, set the timer, and let the Ninja Max do its job. The cook & crisp basket is great for cooking vegetables, fish, and chicken. For best results, place your food in the basket and then add water to the pot until it reaches the "max fill" line. Sauteing is a quick and easy way to cook a tasty meal. To use the saute function, simply add oil to the pot and then press the "saute". Simply add your desired ingredients to the basket, then

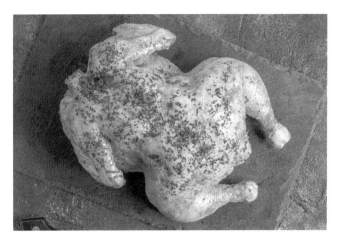

place it in the cooker pot. The silicone lid is perfect for sealing in moisture and flavors while cooking. It's also dishwasher-safe for easy cleanup. The removable cooking pot is durable and perfect for browning or sautéing ingredients before slow cooking. The recipe book that comes with the Ninja Max Multi Cooker is packed with delicious and easy-to-follow recipes. Be sure to check it out for ideas on what to make. The keep-warm function on the Ninja Max Multi Cooker will keep food warm.

Accessories for Purchase

There are a few different accessories that you can purchase for your Ninja Max Multi Cooker.

Cooking Pot
An extra pot so you can keep the Foodi® fun going when your other pot is already full of delicious food.

Multi-Purpose Silicone Sling
Easily lift ingredients and pans into and out of the cooking pot.

Multi-Purpose Tin
Create casseroles, dips, and sweet and savory pies, or bake a fluffy, moist cake with a golden top for dessert. D22cm H6cm.

Folding Crisping Rack
Cook an entire pack of bacon or turn tortillas into taco shells

Loaf Tin
Our specially designed pan is the perfectly sized baking accessory for bread mixes like banana and courgette. L21cm x W11cm x H9cm approx.

Glass Lid
See into the pot during multiple cooking functions, then use to transport or store easily.

Extra Pack of Silicone Rings
2-pack silicone ring set helps keep flavours separate—use one when cooking savory foods and the other when cooking sweet foods

Skewer Stand
Only compatible with the 7.5L models. Use the skewer stand to create kebabs. 15 skewers included.

Cleaning and Caring for Ninja Foodi MAX Multi-Cooker

First and foremost, unplug your cooker from the outlet. You don't want to be electrocuted while cleaning! Next, remove all removable parts from the cooker. This includes the cooking pot, lid, air fryer basket, and any other attachments. Wash all of the removable parts in warm, soapy water. Be sure to scrub any stubborn stains. Once the removable parts are clean, it's time to focus on the cooker itself. Use a damp cloth to wipe down the interior and exterior of the cooker. Finally, give the cooker a good once-over with a dry cloth.

Make sure all water is removed, as this could lead to electrical issues. And that's it! You've now successfully cleaned your Ninja Foodi Max Multi Cooker. Below are some tips on how to care for it:
• Wash the removable cooking pot and lid in the dishwasher or by hand with warm soapy water. Do not use abrasive cleaners or scrubbers on the cooking pot as this can damage the nonstick coating.
• The Ninja Foodi Max Multi-Cooker has a stainless steel exterior. Wipe it down with a damp cloth as needed. Do not use abrasive cleaners or scrubbers on the stainless steel as this can damage the finish.
• The control panel is not waterproof, so be careful not to get it wet. If it does get wet, wipe it down with a dry cloth as soon as possible.
• The heating element is located in the base of the Ninja Foodi Max Multi-Cooker. Do not submerge the base in water as this can damage the heating element.

Cleaning: Dishwasher & Hand

If you have a dishwasher, you know the importance of keeping it clean. With all of the different parts and pieces that make up a dishwasher, it can be difficult to know where to start. Luckily, we've got you covered. Here are a few tips to help you keep your dishwasher clean and running smoothly. One of the most important parts of your dishwasher is the filter. Over time, the filter can become clogged with food and grease, which can impact the performance of your dishwasher. Be sure to clean your filter regularly to ensure your dishwasher is running at its best. In addition to the filter, the spray arm is another important part of your dishwasher. The spray arm is responsible for spraying water and detergent onto your dishes. If the spray arm becomes clogged, it can impact the performance of your dishwasher. Be sure to check the spray arm regularly and clean it as needed.

Removing and Reinstalling the Silicon Ring

If you own a Ninja Max Multi Cooker, you know that it's a versatile appliance that can help you create delicious meals. But

one thing that can be a bit of a pain is removing the silicon ring when it's time to clean the pot. Luckily, there's an easy way to do it! To remove the silicon ring, simply twist it counterclockwise until it comes loose. Once it's loose, you can pull it off the pot and wash it in the sink. If you're having trouble getting a grip on the ring, you can use a butter knife or a small spatula to help pry it off. Once the ring is off, you can wash the pot as usual. Be sure to dry it thoroughly before putting the silicon ring back on. When you're ready to use the pot again, simply twist the ring clockwise to secure it in place. Now you know how to easily remove and replace the silicon ring. If your Ninja Max Multi Cooker isn't working correctly, one troubleshooting step you can try is to reinstall the silicon ring. Here's a quick guide on how to do that:
• Unplug the cooker from the outlet.
• Remove the pot from the cooker.
• Carefully remove the silicon ring from the pot. You may need to use a small knife or other tools to help pry it off.
• Clean the pot and ring with warm, soapy water.
• Rinse the pot and ring well and dry completely.
• Place the silicon ring back on the pot, making sure it's seated correctly.
• Place the pot back in the cooker.
• Plug the cooker back in and try again.

Frequently Asked Questions

If you're like most people, you probably have a lot of questions about the Ninja Foodi Max Multi Cooker. Here are some of the most frequently asked questions about this amazing kitchen appliance:

What can the Ninja Foodi Max Multi Cooker do?
The Ninja Foodi Max Multi Cooker is a versatile kitchen appliance that can do it all. It can pressure cook, slow cook, air fry, steam, sear, and more. If you can think of it, the Ninja Foodi Max can probably do it.

How big is the Ninja Foodi Max Multi-Cooker?
The Ninja Foodi Max Multi Cooker is big enough to feed a family

of four. It has a 6.5-quart capacity cooking pot and a 5-quart capacity air fryer basket.

How much does the Ninja Foodi Max Multi-Cooker cost?
The Ninja Foodi Max Multi Cooker is very reasonably priced.

Troubleshooting Guide

If you're having trouble with your Ninja Max Multi Cooker, here's a troubleshooting guide to help you get back on track. First, make sure that the cooker is properly plugged in and that the power switch is in the "on" position. If the cooker still doesn't seem to be working, try resetting it by unplugging it for a few seconds and then plugging it back in. If the cooker is still not working, the next step is to check the lid. Make sure that the lid is properly seated on the cooker and that the sealing ring is in place. If the lid is not sealing properly, the cooker will not come under pressure and will not work properly. If the lid is sealed and the cooker is still not working, the next step is to check the pressure release valve. Make sure that the valve is in the "sealing" position.

Helpful Tips

Are you the proud owner of a Ninja Foodi Max Multi-Cooker? If so, congratulations! You now have a powerful, versatile kitchen appliance that can help you create delicious, healthy meals for your family. Here are a few helpful tips to get the most out of your Ninja Foodi Max:
• Use the pre-heat function to get the perfect cooking temperature.
• When cooking meat, poultry, or fish, be sure to use the sear/sauté function to seal in juices and flavor.
• Use the slow cook function to create tender, flavorful dishes without having to watch them closely.

• The steam function is perfect for cooking vegetables and rice.
• The bake function can be used to create delicious, healthy desserts.
• The keep-warm function is perfect for keeping food warm until everyone is ready to eat.
• The delay start function is perfect for busy families

Replacement parts

If you need replacement parts for your Ninja Foodi Max Multi Cooker, you've come to the right place. Here at Ninja, we know that sometimes things break and that's why we offer a wide variety of replacement parts for our products. Whether you need a new lid, pot, or even just a new seal, we've got you covered. If you're unsure of which replacement part you need, our team of experts is always ready to help. Simply contact us and we'll be happy to assist you in finding the perfect replacement for your Ninja Foodi Max Multi Cooker.

Product Registration

It's important to register your Ninja Foodi Max Multi Cooker so you can receive the full warranty and other benefits that come with owning one of these amazing devices. Here's how to register your Ninja Foodi Max Multi-Cooker:
• Visit the Ninja website and create an account.
• Once you've created an account, log in and click on the "Register a Product" link.
• Enter the serial number of your Ninja Foodi Max Multi Cooker.
• Fill out the rest of the required information and click "Submit."
• That's it! You've now registered your Ninja Foodi Max Multi Cooker.

4-Week Meal Plan

Week 1

Day 1:
Breakfast: Traditional Shakshuka
Lunch: Cheesy Mushroom and Herb Risotto
Snack: Hoisin Meatballs with Sesame Seeds
Dinner: elicious Chicken & Sausage Jambalaya
Dessert: Cinnamon Brown Rice Raisins Pudding

Day 2:
Breakfast: Cheese Ham Strata
Lunch: Sour Cream Cabbage
Snack: Caribbean Chipotle Pork Sliders with Coleslaw
Dinner: Gingered Chicken with Rice & Mushrooms
Dessert: Rice Cream Pudding

Day 3:
Breakfast: Greens & Eggs in a Boat
Lunch: Italian Sausage and Rocket Risotto
Snack: Spicy Dill Deviled Eggs
Dinner: Homemade BBQ Apricot Pulled Pork
Dessert: Vanilla Banana Bread

Day 4:
Breakfast: Cheesy Eggs with Jalapeño
Lunch: Vegetarian Red Kidney Beans & Brown Rice
Snack: Juicy Pulled Pork Sliders
Dinner: Pork & Chicken Noodles
Dessert: Walnuts-Oats Stuffed Apples

Day 5:
Breakfast: Toast with Sweet & Spicy Tomato Jam
Lunch: Herbed Carrots & Parsnips
Snack: Sour Cream Deviled Eggs with Olives
Dinner: Flavourful Chicken Vindaloo with Potatoes
Dessert: Traditional Peach Cobbler

Day 6:
Breakfast: Fresh Blueberries & Cream Clafouti
Lunch: Mushroom, Peas & Barley "Risotto"
Snack: Turkey Cabbage Dumplings
Dinner: Cheesesteak Mushroom Sloppy Joes
Dessert: Cinnamon Apples with Dates

Day 7:
Breakfast: Raspberry Breakfast Cake
Lunch: Thyme Celery Root–Cauliflower Mash with Caramelized Onion
Snack: Parmesan Crab and Courgette Dip
Dinner: Lime Carnitas Tacos with Avocado Crema
Dessert: Red Wine Braised Pears

Week 2

Day 1:
Breakfast: Chocolate Banana Bread
Lunch: Lemon-Garlic Smashed Red Potatoes
Snack: Prawns with Thai-Style Sauce
Dinner: Smoky & Spicy Broiled Chicken Breasts
Dessert: Sweet Cranberry Applesauce

Day 2:
Breakfast: Cinnamon Steel Cut Oats with Raisins
Lunch: Cheese Corned Beef & Cabbage Slaw
Snack: Chinese Spiced Chicken Wings
Dinner: Salsa Verde Pulled Pork with Coriander
Dessert: Lemon Blueberry Compote

Day 3:
Breakfast: Creamy Vanilla Peaches Steel Cut Oats
Lunch: Herbed Veggie & Bread Casserole
Snack: Pickle Deviled Eggs
Dinner: Smoked Brisket Skewers
Dessert: Cinnamon Dried Fruit Compote

Day 4:
Breakfast: Maple Steel-Cut Oatmeal with Fruit
Lunch: Red Wine Braised Mushroom
Snack: Classic Aubergine Dip
Dinner: Herbed Pomegranate Chicken
Dessert: Delicious Chocolate Rice Pudding

Day 5:
Breakfast: Almond & Date Oatmeal
Lunch: Buttered Mashed Potatoes
Snack: Healthy Artichokes
Dinner: Smoky Corned Beef with Potatoes
Dessert: Banana Pecans Pudding Cake

Day 6:
Breakfast: Maple Quinoa, Blueberry & Yogurt Breakfast Bowls
Lunch: Potato Yogurt Salad
Snack: Black-Eyed Peas and Corn Dip
Dinner: Lemon Garlic Chicken
Dessert: Tasty Coconut Cake

Day 7:
Breakfast: Baked Eggs with Creamy Ham & Kale
Lunch: Pecans & Marshmallows Loaded Sweet Potatoes
Snack: Savoy Beef Stuffed Cabbage Rolls
Dinner: Sweet & Sour Beef Short Ribs
Dessert: Apple Crisp with Pecans-Oats Topping

Week 3

Day 1:
Breakfast: Feta &Red Pepper Eggs
Lunch: Lime Cauliflower Rice with Coriander
Snack: Hoisin Meatballs with Sesame Seeds
Dinner: Braised Chuck Roast with Raisins
Dessert: Lemon Pecans Cake with Chickpeas Filling

Day 2:
Breakfast: Herbed Egg Casserole with Kale
Lunch: Courgette and Tomato Bowls
Snack: Caribbean Chipotle Pork Sliders with Coleslaw
Dinner: Creamy Chicken & Peas
Dessert: Apple Cake

Day 3:
Breakfast: Raspberry Steel Cut Oats Bars
Lunch: Asian Mushroom & Sweet Potato Bowls
Snack: Spicy Dill Deviled Eggs
Dinner: Herbed Lamb and Butternut Squash Stew
Dessert: Cinnamon Brown Rice Raisins Pudding

Day 4:
Breakfast: Wild Blueberry and Quinoa Porridge
Lunch: Cheese Potato Onion Pie
Snack: Juicy Pulled Pork Sliders
Dinner: Cheesy Beef and Pasta Casserole
Dessert: Rice Cream Pudding

Day 5:
Breakfast: Orange Banana Oatmeal Muffins
Lunch: Delicious Ranch Potatoes
Snack: Sour Cream Deviled Eggs with Olives
Dinner: Chicken Artichoke Casserole
Dessert: Vanilla Banana Bread

Day 6:
Breakfast: Delicious Coconut Chocolate Oatmeal
Lunch: Herbed Carrots & Parsnips
Snack: Turkey Cabbage Dumplings
Dinner: Gingered Honey Beef Short Ribs
Dessert: Walnuts-Oats Stuffed Apples

Day 7:
Breakfast: Cheesy Eggs with Jalapeño
Lunch: Thyme Celery Root–Cauliflower Mash with Caramelized Onion
Snack: Parmesan Crab and Courgette Dip
Dinner: Beef & Olives Casserole
Dessert: Traditional Peach Cobbler

Week 4

Day 1:
Breakfast: Cheese Ham Strata
Lunch: Sour Cream Cabbage
Snack: Prawns with Thai-Style Sauce
Dinner: Herbed Chicken
Dessert: Cinnamon Apples with Dates

Day 2:
Breakfast: Toast with Sweet & Spicy Tomato Jam
Lunch: Lemon-Garlic Smashed Red Potatoes
Snack: Chinese Spiced Chicken Wings
Dinner: Balsamic Garlic Lamb
Dessert: Red Wine Braised Pears

Day 3:
Breakfast: Fresh Blueberries & Cream Clafouti
Lunch: Cheese Corned Beef & Cabbage Slaw
Snack: Pickle Deviled Eggs
Dinner: Rosemary-Cherry Pork Tenderloin
Dessert: Lemon Blueberry Compote

Day 4:
Breakfast: Chocolate Banana Bread
Lunch: Herbed Veggie & Bread Casserole
Snack: Classic Aubergine Dip
Dinner: Spiced Chicken Wings
Dessert: Cinnamon Dried Fruit Compote

Day 5:
Breakfast: Creamy Vanilla Peaches Steel Cut Oats
Lunch: Red Wine Braised Mushroom
Snack: Savoy Beef Stuffed Cabbage Rolls
Dinner: Pork Chops with Rice & Vegetables
Dessert: Delicious Chocolate Rice Pudding

Day 6:
Breakfast: Almond & Date Oatmeal
Lunch: Buttered Mashed Potatoes
Snack: Black-Eyed Peas and Corn Dip
Dinner: Fried Herbed Chicken Thighs
Dessert: Banana Pecans Pudding Cake

Day 7:
Breakfast: Baked Eggs with Creamy Ham & Kale
Lunch: Pecans & Marshmallows Loaded Sweet Potatoes
Snack: Healthy Artichokes
Dinner: Pork Chops with Mushroom & Tomato Sauce
Dessert: Tasty Coconut Cake

Chapter 1 Breakfast Recipes

Traditional Shakshuka

2 tbsp (30 ml) avocado oil or olive oil

1 small yellow onion, diced

1 green pepper, seeded and diced

1 clove garlic, minced

60 ml water

1 (800-g) can whole tomatoes, with juices

1½ tsp (3.5 g) smoked paprika

½ tsp ground cumin

½ tsp sea salt

4 large eggs

15 g chopped fresh parsley or (10 g) coriander, for serving

3 tbsp (28 g) crumbled feta cheese, for serving (optional)

1. Move slider to AIR FRY/STOVETOP. Select SEAR/SAUTÉ and set to 3. Select START/STOP to begin preheating. Allow unit to preheat for 5 minutes. After 5 minutes, add oil to the bottom of the pot and add the onion and pepper. Sauté for 2 to 3 minutes, then add the garlic. Cook for 1 more minute, or until the vegetables are softened and fragrant. Press START/STOP to turn off the SEAR/SAUTÉ function. 2. Add water to the pot. Then, add the tomatoes with their juices, cumin, paprika and salt. 3. Close the lid and move the slider to PRESSURE. Make sure the pressure release valve is in the SEAL position. The temperature will default to HIGH, which is the correct setting. Set time to 6 minutes. Select START/STOP to begin cooking. 4. When cooking is complete, turn the pressure release valve to the vent position for a quick pressure release. Move slider to the right to unlock the lid, then carefully open it. 5. Gently crack each egg into a ladle or large wooden spoon and slowly lower into the tomato sauce. 6. Close the lid once again, and select PRESSURE and 0 minutes (yes, zero). 7. Use a quick release and remove the lid. You can leave the lid on longer for a more cooked egg. 8. Serve hot with fresh parsley or coriander, and feta cheese.

Per Serving: Calories 396; Fat 28.98g; Sodium 1460mg; Carbs 24.95g; Fibre 9.7g; Sugar 15.43g; Protein 13.79g

Cheese Ham Strata

1 tbsp unsalted butter

250 ml water

6 large eggs

¼ tsp ground cumin

¼ tsp mustard powder

80 ml heavy cream

Salt

Freshly ground black pepper

95 g leftover mole carnitas or store-bought cooked pulled pork

75 g cubed ham

85 g shredded Swiss cheese

100 g cubed French bread

1 small to medium kosher dill pickle, thinly sliced

1. Butter a round baking dish that can fit the pot. Pour water into the pot and place the Deluxe Reversible Rack in the lower position in the pot. 2. Combine together the eggs, cumin, cream, mustard powder, salt and pepper in a bowl. 3. Stir in the mole carnitas, Swiss, ham, bread and pickle. Let the mixture sit for 2 minutes and then transfer to the prepared baking dish. 4. Carefully place the baking dish on the rack in the pot. 5. Close the lid and move the slider to PRESSURE. Make sure the pressure release valve is in the SEAL position. The temperature will default to HIGH, which is the correct setting. Set time to 20 minutes. Select START/STOP to begin cooking. 6. When cooking is complete, turn the pressure release valve to the vent position for a quick pressure release. Move slider to the right to unlock the lid, then carefully open it. 7. Lift the rack and baking dish out of the pot. Let the strata cool slightly before slicing.

Per Serving: Calories 362; Fat 23.18g; Sodium 716mg; Carbs 18.02g; Fibre 0.9g; Sugar 6.49g; Protein 19.84g

Greens & Eggs in a Boat

Prep Time: 15 minutes | Cook Time: 5 minutes | Serves: 6

120 ml water

3 to 4 demi-baguettes

15 g mixed fresh baby spinach and rocket

6 grape tomatoes, halved

6 to 8 large eggs

Salt

Freshly ground black pepper

Crushed red pepper flakes

1. Pour the water into the pot and place the Deluxe Reversible Rack in the lower position in the pot. 2. Cut each demi-baguette to create a lid and well in the bread. Slice length-wise from end to end at a 45-degree angle about three-quarters of the way through the bread. Use your fingers to pull the "lid" off the baguette. Remove any stray pieces of bread from inside the well. Ensuring there is enough room for the eggs. 3. To each demi-baguette, add a few leaves of spinach and rocket along with a few tomato halves. Crack 2 eggs into each bread boat. Top with salt, black pepper and a tiny pinch of red pepper flakes. 4. Arrange up to three bread boats inside the pot on top of the rack. 5. Close the lid and move the slider to PRESSURE. Make sure the pressure release valve is in the SEAL position. The temperature will default to HIGH, which is the correct setting. Set time to 4 minutes. Select START/STOP to begin cooking. 6. When cooking is complete, naturally release the pressure for 3 minutes. Then quick release pressure by turning the pressure release valve to the VENT position. Move slider to AIR FRY/ STOVETOP to unlock the lid, then carefully open it. 7. Remove the boats with tongs and transfer to a plate. Allow the boats to cool for a minute or two so the bread will harden up a bit again, before slicing and serving.

Per Serving: Calories 151; Fat 8.9g; Sodium 392mg; Carbs 9.47g; Fibre 1g; Sugar 3.9g; Protein 8.27g

Cheesy Eggs with Jalapeño

Prep Time: 15 minutes | Cook Time: 10 minutes | Serves: 3

6 large eggs

115 g full-fat cottage cheese

60 g Mexican-blend shredded cheese

1 jalapeño pepper, minced

1 green onion, minced

240 ml water

1. In a high-powered blender, pulse all the ingredients except the water. 2. Pour the water into the pot and place the bottom layer of the Deluxe Reversible Rack in the lower position in the pot. Evenly divide the egg mixture among the wells of a six-bite egg mold. 3. Carefully lower the mold onto the rack. 4. Close the lid and move the slider to PRESSURE. Make sure the pressure release valve is in the SEAL position. The temperature will default to HIGH, which is the correct setting. Set time to 10 minutes. Select START/STOP to begin cooking. 5. When cooking is complete, naturally release the pressure for 10 minutes. Then quick release pressure by turning the pressure release valve to the VENT position. Move slider to AIR FRY/ STOVETOP to unlock the lid, then carefully open it. 6. Carefully remove the eggs from the molds and serve immediately.

Per Serving: Calories 247; Fat 17.32g; Sodium 86mg; Carbs 8.57g; Fibre 1.8g; Sugar 2.7g; Protein 15.04g

Toast with Sweet & Spicy Tomato Jam

Prep Time: 10 minutes | Cook Time: 10 minutes | Serves: 6

455 g tomatoes, cut into eighths
100 g sugar
60 ml white wine vinegar
¼ to ½ tsp crushed red pepper flakes

¼ tsp salt
15 ml water
Toast or crackers, for serving

1. In the pot, mix together all the ingredients except the toast. 2. Close the lid and move the slider to PRESSURE. Make sure the pressure release valve is in the SEAL position. The temperature will default to HIGH, which is the correct setting. Set time to 10 minutes. Select START/STOP to begin cooking. 3. When the timer beeps, quick release the pressure. 4. Open the lid and use a potato masher to mash the tomatoes into small pieces. As the jam cools, it will thicken. 5. When the jam is completely cool, transfer to a pint-size Mason jar with a lid. Store in the refrigerator for up to 3 weeks. 6. Spread the jam on toast or crackers.
Per Serving: Calories 51; Fat 0.17g; Sodium 130mg; Carbs 11.63g; Fibre 0.8g; Sugar 8.29g; Protein 1.02g

Fresh Blueberries & Cream Clafouti

Prep Time: 5 minutes | Cook Time: 15 minutes | Serves: 2

Butter, at room temperature, for greasing
3 tablespoons granulated sugar, plus more for sprinkling
80 g fresh blueberries
1 egg
1 tablespoon plain flour
1 teaspoon rum

60 g heavy cream
60 ml whole milk
¼ teaspoon grated lemon zest
¼ teaspoon vanilla extract
Pinch salt
Icing sugar, for garnish

1. Pour 240 ml of water into the pot and place the bottom layer of the Deluxe Reversible Rack in the lower position in the pot. 2. Butter two ramekins, then sprinkle a bit of granulated sugar in each of them and tip to coat. Divide the blueberries between the ramekins, set aside. 3. In a medium bowl, whisk the egg and 3 tablespoons of granulated sugar until well combined. Stir in the flour, rum, cream, milk, vanilla, lemon zest, and salt for about 1 minute until smooth. Pour the batter over the berries, filling the ramekins about three-quarters full. 4. Put the ramekins on the rack and place a square of aluminum foil loosely on top. 5. Close the lid and move the slider to PRESSURE. Make sure the pressure release valve is in the SEAL position. The temperature will default to HIGH, which is the correct setting. Set time to 11 minutes. Select START/STOP to begin cooking. 6. When cooking is complete, quick release the pressure in the pot. 7. Move slider to AIR FRY/STOVETOP position. Select BROIL and set time to 4 minutes, Select START/STOP to begin cooking. 8. The top should be browned, then transfer to a cooling rack and let cool for 10 to 15 minutes. Garnish with icing sugar and serve.
Per Serving: Calories 290; Fat 13.7g; Sodium 228mg; Carbs 34.69g; Fibre 1.1g; Sugar 27.22g; Protein 6.52g

Raspberry Breakfast Cake

120 g plain flour, plus more for dusting and coating

55 g unsalted butter, at room temperature, plus more for greasing

1 teaspoon baking powder

¼ teaspoon salt

65 g granulated sugar

1 egg, at room temperature

½ teaspoon vanilla extract

½ teaspoon almond extract

60 ml buttermilk

160 g fresh raspberries

Icing sugar, for garnish (optional)

1. Add 240 ml of water to the pot and place the bottom layer of the Deluxe Reversible Rack in the lower position in the pot. 2. Coat a 16 cm cake pan with butter and then with flour. Set aside. 3. Mix flour, the baking powder, and the salt in a bowl. Reserve 2 tablespoons of the flour mixture in another small bowl. 4. In a big bowl, mix the granulated sugar and 55 g of butter with an electric hand mixer until well combined, scraping down the sides of the bowl as necessary. 5. Add in the egg, vanilla, and almond extract, mix to combine well. 6. Add the flour mixture and the buttermilk in alternating batches to the batter, mixing well after each addition. 7. In a medium bowl, lightly toss the raspberries with some flour to coat. Gently fold the berries into the cake batter. Pour the batter into the prepared pan and put the pan on the rack in the pressure cooker. 8. Close the lid and move the slider to PRESSURE. Make sure the pressure release valve is in the SEAL position. The temperature will default to HIGH, which is the correct setting. Set time to 30 minutes. Select START/STOP to begin cooking. 9. When cooking is complete, quick release the pressure in the pot, then remove the lid and immediately transfer the cake to a cooling rack. 10. Let cool for 10 to 15 minutes, then dust with powdered sugar (if desired). Serve warm.

Per Serving: Calories 632; Fat 21.44g; Sodium 418mg; Carbs 97.4g; Fibre 6g; Sugar 43.92g; Protein 14.01g

Cinnamon Steel Cut Oats with Raisins

1 tbsp butter

110 g steel oats

840 ml water

A pinch of salt

100 g raisins

2 tbsp white sugar

50 g cream cheese, soft

1 tsp milk

1 tsp cinnamon

60 g brown sugar

1. Move slider to AIR FRY/STOVETOP. Select SEAR/SAUTÉ and set to 2. Select START/STOP to begin preheating. Allow unit to preheat for 5 minutes. After 5 minutes, add butter and melt it. 2. Stir in oats and sauté for 3 minutes. Add a pinch of salt and water. Press START/STOP to turn off the SEAR/SAUTÉ function. 3. Close the lid and move the slider to PRESSURE. Make sure the pressure release valve is in the SEAL position. The temperature will default to HIGH, which is the correct setting. Set time to 10 minutes. Select START/STOP to begin cooking. 4. When cooking is complete, naturally release the pressure for 5 minutes. Then quick release pressure by turning the pressure release valve to the VENT position. Move slider to AIR FRY/ STOVETOP to unlock the lid, then carefully open it. 5. Stir in the raisins and set aside. 6. In the meantime, mix white sugar with cream cheese and milk and stir well. 7. In another bowl, mix cinnamon with brown sugar and stir. 8. Transfer oats mix to breakfast bowls and top each with cinnamon mix and cream cheese one. Serve.

Per Serving: Calories 196; Fat 8.64g; Sodium 240mg; Carbs 34.2g; Fibre 4g; Sugar 18.23g; Protein 5.19g

Creamy Vanilla Peaches Steel Cut Oats

Prep Time: 10 minutes | Cook Time: 3 minutes | Serves: 4

2 peaches, diced
80 g steel cut oats
240 ml coconut milk, full fat

480 ml water
½ vanilla bean, scraped, seeds and pod

1. Combine all the ingredients in the pressure cooker pot. 2. Close the lid and move the slider to PRESSURE. Make sure the pressure release valve is in the SEAL position. The temperature will default to HIGH, which is the correct setting. Set time to 3 minutes. Select START/STOP to begin cooking. 3. When cooking is complete, naturally release the pressure for 10 minutes. Then quick release pressure by turning the pressure release valve to the VENT position. Move slider to AIR FRY/ STOVETOP to unlock the lid, then carefully open it. 4. Sweeten the oats, if desired. Serve.

Per Serving: Calories 125; Fat 3.84g; Sodium 30mg; Carbs 25.77g; Fibre 4.8g; Sugar 9.79g; Protein 6.73g

Chocolate Banana Bread

Prep Time: 10 minutes | Cook Time: 40 minutes | Serves: 2

3 tablespoons unsalted butter, at room temperature, plus more for greasing
60 g applesauce
2 tablespoons packed brown sugar
1 egg, at room temperature
2 very ripe bananas, mashed

60 ml milk
½ teaspoon vanilla extract
125 g flour
1 teaspoon baking soda
¼ teaspoon Salt
45 g chocolate chips

1. Add 240 ml to the pressure cooker pot and place the Deluxe Reversible Rack in the lower position in the pot. 2. Coat a 16-cm loaf pan with butter, set aside. 3. Combine together 3 tablespoons of butter, the applesauce, and the brown sugar in a medium bowl. Add the egg and stir in the mashed bananas, milk, and vanilla. 4. Stir in the flour, salt and baking soda. Fold in the chocolate chips. Pour the batter into the prepared loaf pan and cover with foil, then place on the rack inside the pot. 5. Close the lid and move the slider to PRESSURE. Make sure the pressure release valve is in the SEAL position. The temperature will default to HIGH, which is the correct setting. Set time to 40 minutes. Select START/STOP to begin cooking. 6. When cooking is complete, naturally release the pressure for 10 minutes. Then quick release pressure by turning the pressure release valve to the VENT position. Move slider to AIR FRY/ STOVETOP to unlock the lid, then carefully open it. 7. Carefully remove the pan and place on a cooling rack. Remove the foil, being sure to avoid dripping any condensation onto the bread. 8. Test the bread with a toothpick to make sure the centre is fully cooked; no more than a few moist crumbs should be on the toothpick. End with a quick release. Let cool at room temperature for at least 45 minutes. 9. Once the banana bread has thoroughly cooled, cut into thick slices.

Per Serving: Calories 751; Fat 32.35g; Sodium 1100mg; Carbs 101.85g; Fibre 5.4g; Sugar 33.58g; Protein 15.33g

Maple Steel-Cut Oatmeal with Fruit

Prep Time: 15 minutes | Cook Time: 6 minutes | Serves: 2

720 g water, divided
80 g toasted steel-cut oats
2 teaspoons unsalted butter
240 ml apple juice
1 tablespoon dried cranberries

1 tablespoon golden raisins
1 tablespoon snipped dried apricots
1 tablespoon maple syrup
¼ teaspoon ground cinnamon
⅛ teaspoon salt

1. Pour 120 ml water into the pot and place the bottom layer of the Deluxe Reversible Rack in the lower position in the pot. Fold a long piece of aluminum foil in half lengthwise. Lay foil over rack to form a sling. 2. In a metal bowl that fits the inside of the pot, add remaining water, apple juice, oats, butter, cranberries, apricots, raisins, maple syrup, cinnamon, and salt. Stir to combine well. Place bowl on the rack in the pot so it rests on the sling. 3. Close the lid and move the slider to PRESSURE. Make sure the pressure release valve is in the SEAL position. The temperature will default to HIGH, which is the correct setting. Set time to 6 minutes. Select START/STOP to begin cooking. 4. When the timer beeps, let pressure release naturally, about 20 minutes. Open lid and carefully lift bowl out of the pot using the sling. Spoon the cooked oats into bowls. Serve warm.
Per Serving: Calories 173; Fat 3.7g; Sodium 172mg; Carbs 39.08g; Fibre 3.6g; Sugar 23.31g; Protein 3.92g

Almond & Date Oatmeal

Prep Time: 15 minutes | Cook Time: 12 minutes | Serves: 4

120 g sliced almonds
960 ml water
160 g rolled oats

1 tablespoon extra-virgin olive oil
¼ teaspoon salt
65 g chopped pitted dates

1. Move slider to AIR FRY/STOVETOP. Select SEAR/SAUTÉ and set to 3. Select START/STOP to begin preheating. Allow unit to preheat for 5 minutes. After 5 minutes, add almonds and stir constantly, until almonds are golden brown, about 8 minutes. Press START/STOP to turn off the SEAR/SAUTÉ function. 2. Add water, oats, salt, oil, and dates to the pot. Stir well. 3. Close the lid and move the slider to PRESSURE. Make sure the pressure release valve is in the SEAL position. The temperature will default to HIGH, which is the correct setting. Set time to 4 minutes. Select START/STOP to begin cooking. 4. When the timer beeps, quick-release the pressure until the float valve drops, open the lid, and stir well. Serve hot.
Per Serving: Calories 183; Fat 5.03g; Sodium 182mg; Carbs 44.97g; Fibre 8.7g; Sugar 12.34g; Protein 9.66g

Maple Quinoa, Blueberry & Yogurt Breakfast Bowls

Prep Time: 15 minutes | Cook Time: 12 minutes | Serves: 8

360 g quinoa, rinsed and drained
960 ml water
1 teaspoon vanilla extract
¼ teaspoon salt

480 g low-fat plain Greek yogurt
325 g blueberries
120 g toasted almonds
55 g pure maple syrup

1. Add quinoa, vanilla, water, and salt to the pot, stir well. Close the lid and move the slider to PRESSURE. Make sure the pressure release valve is in the SEAL position. The temperature will default to HIGH, which is the correct setting. Set time to 12 minutes. Select START/STOP to begin cooking. 2. When the timer beeps, let pressure release naturally, about 20 minutes. Open lid and fluff quinoa with a fork. 3. Stir in yogurt. Serve warm, topped with berries, almonds, and maple syrup.
Per Serving: Calories 305; Fat 3.83g; Sodium 124mg; Carbs 59g; Fibre 4g; Sugar 29.38g; Protein 9.67g

Baked Eggs with Creamy Ham & Kale

Prep Time: 15 minutes | Cook Time: 25 minutes | Serves: 6

1 tablespoon olive oil
200 g diced ham
1 medium yellow onion, peeled and chopped
900 g chopped kale
120 g heavy cream
1 (200 g) package cream cheese

¼ teaspoon salt
¼ teaspoon ground black pepper
⅛ teaspoon ground nutmeg
6 large eggs
240 ml water

1. Spray a round baking dish that fits the inside of the pot with nonstick cooking spray. 2. Move slider to AIR FRY/ STOVETOP. Select SEAR/SAUTÉ and set to 3. Select START/STOP to begin preheating. Allow unit to preheat for 5 minutes. After 5 minutes, heat the oil, then add ham. Cook until ham starts to brown, about 5 minutes. Add onion and cook until tender, about 5 minutes, then add kale and cook until wilted, about 5 minutes. 3. Add cream cheese, cream, salt, pepper, and nutmeg, and stir until the cream cheese is melted and the mixture thickens, about 5 minutes. Press START/STOP to turn off the SEAR/SAUTÉ function. Transfer the mixture to the prepared baking dish. Clean out the pot. 4. Use a spoon to press six indentations into kale mixture. Crack eggs into indentations. 5. Add water to the pot. Then place the bottom layer of the Deluxe Reversible Rack in the lower position in the pot. 6. Fold a long piece of aluminum foil in half lengthwise. Lay foil over rack to form a sling. Place dish on rack so it rests on the sling and cover loosely with aluminum foil to protect eggs from condensation inside pot. 7. Close the lid and move the slider to PRESSURE. Make sure the pressure release valve is in the SEAL position. The temperature will default to HIGH, which is the correct setting. Set time to 5 minutes. Select START/STOP to begin cooking. 8. When cooking is complete, naturally release the pressure for 10 minutes. Then quick release pressure by turning the pressure release valve to the VENT position. Move slider to AIR FRY/ STOVETOP to unlock the lid, then carefully open it. 9. Let stand for 5 minutes before carefully removing dish from pot with sling. Serve warm.
Per Serving: Calories 372; Fat 25.56g; Sodium 917mg; Carbs 17.89g; Fibre 5.8g; Sugar 6.54g; Protein 22.12g

Feta &Red Pepper Eggs

Prep Time: 15 minutes | Cook Time: 8 minutes | Serves: 6

1 tablespoon olive oil

60 g crumbled feta cheese

35 g chopped roasted red peppers

6 large eggs, beaten

¼ teaspoon ground black pepper

240 ml water

1. Brush inside of the poaching cups with oil. Divide feta and roasted red peppers among the prepared cups. In a bowl with a pour spout, whisk the eggs with black pepper. 2. Add water to the pot. Then place the bottom layer of the Deluxe Reversible Rack in the lower position in the pot. 3. Pour the egg mixture into cups and place the cups on the rack in the pot. 4. Close the lid and move the slider to PRESSURE. Make sure the pressure release valve is in the SEAL position. The temperature will default to HIGH, which is the correct setting. Set time to 8 minutes. Select START/STOP to begin cooking. 5. When cooking is complete, turn the pressure release valve to the vent position for a quick pressure release. Move slider to the right to unlock the lid, then carefully open it. 6. Remove silicone cups carefully and slide eggs from cups onto plates. Serve warm.

Per Serving: Calories 110; Fat 9.44g; Sodium 124mg; Carbs 1.68g; Fibre 0.1g; Sugar 0.95g; Protein 4.56g

Herbed Egg Casserole with Kale

Prep Time: 15 minutes | Cook Time: 17 minutes | Serves: 6

1 tablespoon avocado oil

1 small yellow onion, peeled and chopped

5 large kale leaves, tough stems removed and finely chopped

1 clove garlic, diced

2 tablespoons lemon juice

½ teaspoon salt, divided

9 large eggs

2 tablespoons water

1½ teaspoons dried rosemary

1 teaspoon dried oregano

¼ teaspoon black pepper

50 g nutritional yeast

1. Add the oil to the pot, move slider to AIR FRY/STOVETOP. Select SEAR/SAUTÉ and set to 3. Select START/STOP to begin cooking, heat the oil for 1 minute. 2. Add the onion and sauté 2 minutes until just softened. 3. Stir in the kale, garlic, lemon juice, and ¼ teaspoon salt, cook for 2 minutes more. Press START/STOP to turn off the SEAR/SAUTÉ function. 4. Meanwhile, whisk together the eggs, water, oregano, rosemary, ¼ teaspoon salt, pepper, and nutritional yeast in a medium bowl. 5. Add the onion and kale mixture to the egg mixture and stir to combine well. 6. Clean the pot and add 480 ml water. Then place the bottom layer of the Deluxe Reversible Rack in the lower position in the pot. 7. Spray a springform pan with cooking spray. Transfer the egg mixture to the springform pan. 8. Place the pan on the rack and close the lid. move slider to PRESSURE and make sure the pressure release valve is in the SEAL position. The temperature will default to HIGH, which is the correct setting. Set time to 12 minutes. Select START/STOP to begin cooking. 9. When cooking is complete, turn the pressure release valve to the vent position for a quick pressure release. Move slider to the right to unlock the lid, then carefully open it. 10. Remove the pan from the pot and allow to cool 5 minutes before slicing and serving.

Per Serving: Calories 156; Fat 9.39g; Sodium 919mg; Carbs 7.88g; Fibre 2g; Sugar 1.22g; Protein 10.1g

Raspberry Steel Cut Oats Bars

Prep Time: 15 minutes | Cook Time: 15 minutes | Serves: 6

240 g steel cut oats
3 large eggs
480 ml unsweetened vanilla almond milk
40 g erythritol

1 teaspoon pure vanilla extract
¼ teaspoon salt
130 g frozen raspberries

1. In a medium bowl, mix together all ingredients except the raspberries until well combined, fold in the raspberries. 2. Spray a cake pan that fits the pot with cooking oil. Transfer the oat mixture to the pan. Cover the pan with aluminum foil. 3. Pour 240 ml water into the pot and place the Deluxe Reversible Rack in the lower position in the pot. Place the pan with the oat mixture on top of the rack. Close the lid. 4. Move slider to PRESSURE and make sure the pressure release valve is in the SEAL position. The temperature will default to HIGH, which is the correct setting. Set time to 15 minutes. Select START/ STOP to begin cooking. 5 Press the Manual or Pressure Cook button and adjust the time to 15 minutes. 6. When cooking is complete, turn the pressure release valve to the vent position for a quick pressure release. Move slider to the right to unlock the lid, then carefully open it. 7. Carefully remove the pan from the inner pot and remove the foil. Allow to cool completely before cutting into bars and serving.

Per Serving: Calories 298; Fat 7.92g; Sodium 175mg; Carbs 62.44g; Fibre 9.1g; Sugar 29.78g; Protein 12.69g

Wild Blueberry and Quinoa Porridge

Prep Time: 15 minutes | Cook Time: 1 minute | Serves: 4

135 g dry quinoa
720 ml water
130 g frozen wild blueberries

½ teaspoon pure stevia powder
1 teaspoon pure vanilla extract

1. Rinse the quinoa very well until the water runs clear. 2. Add the quinoa, blueberries, water, stevia, and vanilla to the pot. Stir to combine. Close the lid and move the slider to PRESSURE. 3. Make sure the pressure release valve is in the SEAL position. The temperature will default to HIGH, which is the correct setting. Set time to 1 minute. Select START/STOP to begin cooking. 4. When cooking is complete, turn the pressure release valve to the vent position for a quick pressure release. Move slider to the right to unlock the lid, then carefully open it. 5. Allow the quinoa to cool slightly before spooning into bowls to serve.

Per Serving: Calories 258; Fat 3.93g; Sodium 8mg; Carbs 45.94g; Fibre 6g; Sugar 2.63g; Protein 9.01g

Orange Banana Oatmeal Muffins

Prep Time: 10 minutes | Cook Time: 15 minutes | Serves: 6

240 g old fashioned rolled oats
1 teaspoon baking powder
¼ teaspoon salt
1 teaspoon ground cinnamon
60 ml unsweetened vanilla almond milk

60 ml fresh orange juice
300 g mashed bananas
1 large egg
45 g erythritol

1. Add all of the ingredients to a medium bowl and stir until well combined. 2. Place six silicone muffin cups inside of a 15 cm cake pan. Spoon the oatmeal mixture into the muffin cups. Cover the pan with aluminum foil. 3. Pour 240 ml water into the pot and place the bottom layer of the Deluxe Reversible Rack in the lower position in the pot. Place the cake pan with the muffins on the rack. 4. Close the lid and move the slider to PRESSURE. Make sure the pressure release valve is in the SEAL position. The temperature will default to HIGH, which is the correct setting. Set time to 15 minutes. Select START/STOP to begin cooking. 5. When cooking is complete, turn the pressure release valve to the vent position for a quick pressure release. Move slider to the right to unlock the lid, then carefully open it. 6. Carefully remove the pan from the pot and remove the foil from the top. Let the muffins cool 15 minutes before eating. They will become firmer as they cool.
Per Serving: Calories 344; Fat 5.19g; Sodium 109mg; Carbs 86.97g; Fibre 13.1g; Sugar 23.52g; Protein 10.87g

Delicious Coconut Chocolate Oatmeal

Prep Time: 15 minutes | Cook Time: 6 minutes | Serves: 4

80 g steel cut oats
1 can full-fat unsweetened coconut milk
480 ml water

50 g cacao powder
50 g erythritol
⅛ teaspoon sea salt

1. Place the oats, cacao powder, coconut milk, erythritol, water, and salt in the pot and stir to combine. 2. Close the lid and move the slider to PRESSURE. Make sure the pressure release valve is in the SEAL position. The temperature will default to HIGH, which is the correct setting. Set time to 6 minutes. Select START/STOP to begin cooking. 3. When cooking is complete, turn the pressure release valve to the vent position for a quick pressure release. Move slider to the right to unlock the lid, then carefully open it. 4. Allow the oatmeal to cool slightly before spooning into bowls to serve.
Per Serving: Calories 359; Fat 26.75g; Sodium 98mg; Carbs 39.81g; Fibre 9g; Sugar 16.08g; Protein 8.29g

Chapter 2 Beans and Grains Recipes

Cheesy Mushroom and Herb Risotto

Prep Time: 20 minutes | Cook Time: 11 minutes | Serves: 4

6 tablespoons salted butter, cut into 1-tablespoon pieces, divided

2 medium shallots, chopped

200 g mixed fresh mushrooms, tough stems removed, thinly sliced

2 tablespoons fresh sage, finely chopped

240 ml vegetable stock, low-sodium

185 g Arborio or carnaroli rice

35 g Parmesan cheese, finely grated ,plus more to serve

4 tablespoons sliced fresh chives (1 cm lengths), divided

4 teaspoons white balsamic vinegar

A pinch of salt and ground black pepper

1. Add 2 tablespoons of the butter to the pot. Move slider to AIR FRY/STOVETOP. Select SEAR/SAUTÉ and set to 3. Select START/STOP to begin cooking. Once the butter has melted, add the shallots and mushrooms, stirring occasionally, cook until the mushrooms have released all of their moisture, about 5 minutes. 2. Add the rice and cook, stirring, until the grains are translucent at the edges, 1 to 2 minutes. Stir in the sage, stock and 360 ml water, then distribute the mixture in an even layer. Press START/STOP to turn off the SEAR/SAUTÉ function. 3. Close the lid and move the slider to PRESSURE. Make sure the pressure release valve is in the SEAL position. Set the heat to LOW and set time to 3 minutes. Select START/STOP to begin cooking. 4. When cooking is complete, turn the pressure release valve to the vent position for a quick pressure release. Move slider to the right to unlock the lid, then carefully open it. 5. Vigorously stir in the Parmesan and the remaining 4 tablespoons butter, adding the butter one piece at a time. Taste and season with salt and pepper, then stir in 3 tablespoons of the chives and the vinegar. 6. Sprinkle with the remaining 1 tablespoon chives. 7. Serve with additional Parmesan on the side.
Per Serving: Calories 436; Fat 21.49g; Sodium 331mg; Carbs 64.86g; Fibre 13.8g; Sugar 5.15g; Protein 13.67g

Italian Sausage and Rocket Risotto

Prep Time: 15 minutes | Cook Time: 10 minutes | Serves: 4

5 tablespoons salted butter, cut into 1-tablespoon pieces, divided

185 g Arborio or carnaroli rice

4 medium garlic cloves, finely chopped

200 g sweet or hot Italian sausage, casing removed, sausage

broken into 1 cm pieces

35 g Parmesan cheese, finely grated, plus more to serve

Salt and ground black pepper

60 g lightly packed baby rocket, roughly chopped

4 teaspoons white balsamic vinegar

1. Add 1 tablespoon of butter to the pot. Move slider to AIR FRY/STOVETOP. Select SEAR/SAUTÉ and set to 3. Select START/STOP to begin cooking. Once the butter is melted, add the rice and garlic, then cook, stirring, until the grains are translucent at the edges, 1 to 2 minutes. 2. Stir in the sausage and 600 ml water, scraping up any browned bits stuck to the bottom of the pot, then distribute the mixture in an even layer. Press START/STOP to turn off the SEAR/SAUTÉ function. 3. Close the lid and move the slider to PRESSURE. Make sure the pressure release valve is in the SEAL position. Set the heat to LOW and set time to 3 minutes. Select START/STOP to begin cooking. 4. When cooking is complete, turn the pressure release valve to the vent position for a quick pressure release. Move slider to the right to unlock the lid, then carefully open it. 5. Stir in the Parmesan, 1 teaspoon pepper and the remaining 4 tablespoons butter, adding the butter one piece at a time. Add the rocket and stir until slightly wilted, about 30 seconds. 6. Taste and season with salt, then stir in the vinegar. Serve sprinkled with pepper and with additional Parmesan on the side.
Per Serving: Calories 325; Fat 23.58g; Sodium 602mg; Carbs 21.02g; Fibre 6.7g; Sugar 2.09g; Protein 17.16g

Simple Garlic Chickpeas

Prep Time: 15 minutes | Cook Time: 25 minutes | Serves: 6

455 g dried chickpeas, rinsed and drained
Salt and ground black pepper
½ teaspoon baking soda

4 medium garlic cloves, smashed and peeled
3 bay leaves

1. Add chickpeas, 2 teaspoons salt, the baking soda and 1.4 L water to the pot, stir to mix well and then distribute in an even layer. 2. Close the lid and move the slider to PRESSURE. Make sure the pressure release valve is in the SEAL position. The temperature will default to HIGH, which is the correct setting. Set time to 5 minutes. Select START/STOP to begin cooking. 3. When cooking is complete, turn the pressure release valve to the vent position for a quick pressure release. Move slider to the right to unlock the lid, then carefully open it. 4. Using potholders, carefully remove the pot from the housing. Drain the chickpeas in a colander; return the pot to the housing. Rinse the chickpeas under cool water, then return them to the pot. Add the garlic, bay and 1.4 L water; stir to combine, then distribute in an even layer. 5. Close the lid and still cook on PRESSURE mode, making sure the pressure release valve is in the SEAL position. The temperature will default to HIGH, which is the correct setting. Set time to 20 minutes. Select START/STOP to begin cooking. 6. When pressure cooking is complete, naturally release the pressure for 20 minutes, then release the remaining steam by moving the pressure valve to Venting. Press START/STOP, then carefully open the pot. 7. Using potholders, carefully remove the pot from the housing and drain the chickpeas in a colander. Remove and discard the bay and garlic. Taste and season with salt and pepper.
Per Serving: Calories 261; Fat 4.13g; Sodium 122mg; Carbs 44.01g; Fibre 8.5g; Sugar 7.54g; Protein 13.99g

Green Beans with Bacon & Toasted Walnuts

Prep Time: 15 minutes | Cook Time: 7 minutes | Serves: 4

5 strips raw bacon, chopped
15 g unsalted butter
60 ml low-sodium chicken stock
340 g washed and trimmed green beans

Salt
Freshly ground black pepper
55 g walnuts

1. Move slider to AIR FRY/STOVETOP. Select SEAR/SAUTÉ and set to 3. Select START/STOP to begin preheating. Allow unit to preheat for 5 minutes. After 5 minutes, add the chopped bacon. Cook for 5 to 6 minutes, or until crispy. 2. Remove the crisp bacon with a slotted spoon. Transfer to a paper towel–lined plate. Press START/STOP. 3. Add the butter and stock to the bacon fat. Use a wooden spoon to scrape up any browned bits from the bottom of the pot. 4. Add the green beans to the pot. Season with salt and pepper. Toss to evenly coat the beans. 5. Close the lid and move the slider to PRESSURE. Make sure the pressure release valve is in the SEAL position. The temperature will default to HIGH, which is the correct setting. Set time to 1 minute. Select START/STOP to begin cooking. 6. In the meantime, heat a small and dry frying pan over medium heat. Add the walnuts and toast them for 2 minutes. Remove from the heat and chop. 7. When cooking is complete, turn the pressure release valve to the vent position for a quick pressure release. Move slider to the right to unlock the lid, then carefully open it. 8. Toss the beans with tongs and transfer the beans and sauce to a plate. Top with the bacon and walnuts.
Per Serving: Calories 151; Fat 13.5g; Sodium 245mg; Carbs 6.3g; Fibre 2.8g; Sugar 1.05g; Protein 4.21g

Cheesy Black Beans and Green Chilies

Prep Time: 15 minutes | Cook Time: 30 minutes | Serves: 8

2 tablespoons olive oil
½ medium yellow onion, peeled and diced
2 cloves garlic, minced
1.4 L vegetable stock
455 g dry black beans
1 (100 g) can mild diced green chilies

1 bay leaf
1 teaspoon cumin
1 teaspoon dried oregano
¼ teaspoon salt
⅛ teaspoon black pepper
200 g shredded sharp Cheddar cheese

1. Add oil to the pot. Move slider to AIR FRY/STOVETOP. Select SEAR/SAUTÉ and set to 3. Select START/STOP to begin cooking. Once the oil is hot, add in onion and cook for 5 minutes, stirring occasionally. 2. Add in garlic and cook for 30 seconds. 3. Pour stock into the pot and deglaze bottom of pot. Press START/STOP to turn off the SEAR/SAUTÉ function. 4. Add in beans, diced green chilies, bay leaf, oregano, cumin, salt, and pepper. 5. Close lid and move slider to PRESSURE. Make sure the pressure release valve is in the SEAL position. The temperature will default to HIGH, which is the correct setting. Set time to 25 minutes. Select START/STOP to begin cooking. 6. When cooking is complete, turn the pressure release valve to the vent position for a quick pressure release. Move slider to the right to unlock the lid, then carefully open it. 7. Stir in cheese. Serve once the cheese is melted.

Per Serving: Calories 417; Fat 15.96g; Sodium 718mg; Carbs 48.16g; Fibre 11.3g; Sugar 4.15g; Protein 22.47g

Garlic Green Beans and Bacon

Prep Time: 10 minutes | Cook Time: 5 minutes | Serves: 6

240 ml water
680 g green beans, ends trimmed
43 g grass-fed butter or ghee

4 cloves garlic, minced
1 tsp sea salt
115 g precooked crispy bacon or turkey bacon, crumbled

1. Pour the water into the pot and place the r Cook & Crisp Basket in the pot. insert a steamer basket. Layer the green beans in the basket. 2. Close the lid and move the slider to PRESSURE. Make sure the pressure release valve is in the SEAL position. The temperature will default to HIGH, which is the correct setting. Set time to 2 minutes. Select START/STOP to begin cooking. 3. When cooking is complete, naturally release the pressure for 10 minutes. Then quick release pressure by turning the pressure release valve to the VENT position. Move slider to AIR FRY/ STOVETOP to unlock the lid, then carefully open it. 4. Carefully remove the green beans and basket, setting the green beans aside. Pour out and discard the water that remains in the pot. 5. Place your healthy fat of choice in the pot and move slider to AIR FRY/STOVETOP. Select SEAR/SAUTÉ and set to 3. Select START/STOP to begin cooking. Once the fat has melted, add the garlic and sauté for 2 minutes, stirring occasionally. 6. Add the green beans back to the pot and stir in the salt and crumbled bacon. Give everything a stir, then sauté for 1 minute to warm the bacon. Press START/STOP. Serve immediately.

Per Serving: Calories 137; Fat 11.87g; Sodium 669mg; Carbs 6.76g; Fibre 2.7g; Sugar 0.91g; Protein 3.48g

Lentils Burger Salad with Special Sauce

Prep Time: 15 minutes | Cook Time: 10 minutes | Serves: 6

Burger "Meat":

1 tablespoon extra-virgin olive oil

1 yellow onion, chopped

1 teaspoon garlic powder

1 teaspoon paprika

⅛ teaspoon cayenne pepper

½ teaspoon ground cumin

¼ teaspoon freshly ground black pepper

150 g green lentils

300 ml water

1 teaspoon fine sea salt

60 g finely chopped raw walnuts

Special Sauce:

60 g raw cashews, soaked for 1 hour

120 ml water

1 tablespoon raw apple cider vinegar

2 tablespoons pure maple syrup

2 tablespoons tomato paste

2 tablespoons yellow mustard

½ teaspoon onion powder

¾ teaspoon fine sea salt

Chopped lettuce, tomatoes, and green onions; pickle slices; and shredded Cheddar cheese, for serving

1. To make the burger "meat," add the olive oil to the pot. Move slider to AIR FRY/STOVETOP. Select SEAR/SAUTÉ and set to 3. Select START/STOP to begin cooking. Once the oil is hot, add the onion and sauté until softened, about 5 minutes. Press START/STOP. 2. Stir in the garlic powder, cumin, cayenne, paprika, and black pepper while the pot is hot. Add the green lentils and water, and stir until the lentils are covered in the liquid for even cooking. 3. Close the lid and move the slider to PRESSURE. Make sure the pressure release valve is in the SEAL position. The temperature will default to HIGH, which is the correct setting. Set time to 5 minutes. Select START/STOP to begin cooking. 4. Meanwhile, make the special sauce. Drain and rinse the cashews, then add them to a blender along with the water, tomato paste, vinegar, mustard, maple syrup, onion powder, and salt. 5. Blend until very smooth, set aside. 6. When the cooking cycle on the burger "meat" is complete, quick release pressure by turning the pressure release valve to the VENT position. Move slider to the right to unlock the lid, then carefully open it. Stir in the salt and chopped walnuts. 7. Fill a bowl with chopped lettuce, the burger "meat," tomatoes, green onions, pickles, and cheese. 8. Drizzle plenty of special sauce over the top before serving. Store leftovers in three separate airtight containers—for the dressing, the burger "meat," and the vegetables—in the fridge for 1 week.

Per Serving: Calories 246; Fat 18.62g; Sodium 829mg; Carbs 18.27g; Fibre 2.3g; Sugar 7.65g; Protein 5.66g

Easy Soaked Beans

Prep Time: 5 minutes | Cook Time: 5 minutes | Serves: 6

455 g dried beans

Water to cover beans

1. Rinse dried beans in a colander and pick out and dispose of any stones. 2. Place the rinsed beans in the pot. Pour into the water until water is 2 cm above top of beans. 3. Close lid and move slider to PRESSURE. Make sure the pressure release valve is in the SEAL position. The temperature will default to HIGH, which is the correct setting. Set time to 5 minutes. Select START/STOP to begin cooking. 4. When cooking is complete, turn the pressure release valve to the vent position for a quick pressure release. Move slider to the right to unlock the lid, then carefully open it and drain out any access water. 5. Store any unused beans in an air-tight container in the refrigerate up to seven days or in the freezer up to three months.

Per Serving: Calories 17; Fat 0.35g; Sodium 2mg; Carbs 3.27g; Fibre 1.4g; Sugar 0.59g; Protein 0.85g

Curried Beans & Broccoli Salad

250 g dried navy beans, soaked for 8 hours

480 ml water

1 head broccoli

1 large carrot

5 green onions, tender white and green parts only

Small handful of fresh coriander

60 g dried cranberries

60 g sliced almonds (optional)

Curried Tahini Dressing:

45 g tahini

60 ml freshly squeezed lemon juice

2 tablespoons pure maple syrup

1 clove garlic, minced

2 teaspoons curry powder

1 teaspoon minced fresh ginger (about 1 cm knob)

1 teaspoon fine sea salt

Freshly ground black pepper

1. Drain the soaked navy beans and add them to the pot with the water. Close the lid and move the slider to PRESSURE. Make sure the pressure release valve is in the SEAL position. The temperature will default to HIGH, which is the correct setting. Set time to 25 minutes. Select START/STOP to begin cooking. 2. Meanwhile, finely chop the broccoli and shred the carrot , adding them to a big mixing bowl. Chop the green onions and coriander, but leave them on the cutting board for now. 3. To make the dressing, in a separate bowl, mix together the tahini, lemon juice, garlic, maple syrup, ginger, curry powder, salt, and black pepper. Whisk well to combine, then add water, 1 tablespoon at a time, and whisk until the dressing is creamy and easy to pour. 4. When the cooking cycle on the beans is complete, naturally release the pressure for 10 minutes. Then quick release pressure by turning the pressure release valve to the VENT position. Move slider to AIR FRY/ STOVETOP to unlock the lid, then carefully open it. 5. Use a fork to mash a bean against the side of the pot to be sure it is tender. If the beans don't mash easily, close the lid and cook at high pressure for 5 minutes more. 6. Let the pressure naturally release for 10 minutes so no foam spurts from the vent, then test the beans for tenderness again. 7. When ready, drain the beans and add them to the bowl with the broccoli and carrots. Stir well and let the beans cool for 15 minutes; the heat from the beans will soften the broccoli slightly. 8. Once cool, stir in the green onions, cranberries, coriander, and almonds and pour the dressing over the top. Toss well to coat evenly. 9. Serve right away, or chill the salad in the fridge for 1 hour to let the flavours meld. Store leftovers in an airtight container in the fridge for 3 days.

Per Serving: Calories 288; Fat 6.6g; Sodium 450mg; Carbs 48.51g; Fibre 11.3g; Sugar 14.4g; Protein 13.65g

Spicy Creamy Black Beans

1.3 kg Simple Black Beans, drained (cooking liquid reserved)

2 tablespoons coconut oil or lard

5 medium garlic cloves, finely chopped

4 teaspoons ground cumin

4 teaspoons ground coriander

1 tablespoon chili powder

Salt and ground black pepper

1. Using a potato masher to mash the beans until mostly smooth. Add 120 ml of the reserved cooking liquid and vigorously stir until the beans are as smooth as possible. 2. Add oil to the pot. Move slider to AIR FRY/STOVETOP. Select SEAR/ SAUTÉ and set to 3. Select START/STOP to begin cooking. Heat the oil until shimmering. Add the cumin, garlic, coriander and chili powder, then cook, stirring occasionally, until fragrant, about 30 seconds. 3. Stir in the mashed beans and cook, stirring frequently, until beginning to brown, 8 to 10 minutes. Continue to cook and stir, adding additional reserved cooking liquid as needed, until the mixture is thick and creamy, about 5 minutes. 4. Taste and season with salt and pepper.

Per Serving: Calories 423; Fat 8.99g; Sodium 65mg; Carbs 65.41g; Fibre 23.6g; Sugar 0.81g; Protein 23.97g

Vegetarian Red Kidney Beans & Brown Rice

Prep Time: 15 minutes | Cook Time: 30 minutes | Serves: 4

220 g dried red kidney beans, soaked for 8 hours
600 ml water
1 yellow onion, chopped
4 celery ribs, chopped
1 red pepper, seeded and chopped
4 cloves garlic, minced
1 teaspoon dried thyme
1 teaspoon dried oregano
⅛ teaspoon cayenne pepper

¼ teaspoon freshly ground black pepper
2 tablespoons tomato paste
185 g long-grain brown rice, rinsed
1 tablespoon soy sauce or tamari
¾ teaspoon fine sea salt
Chopped green onions, tender white and green parts only, for garnish
Chopped fresh coriander, for garnish

1. Pour the drained beans into the pot, add 360 ml of the water, and stir to make sure the beans are submerged for even cooking. Add the onion, celery, red pepper, garlic, oregano, thyme, cayenne, black pepper, and tomato paste on top. 2. Place the Deluxe Reversible Rack in the lower position in the pot and place a 18 cm oven-safe bowl on top. 3. Add the rice and remaining 240 ml water to the bowl. Close the lid and move the slider to PRESSURE. Make sure the pressure release valve is in the SEAL position. The temperature will default to HIGH, which is the correct setting. Set time to 30 minutes. Select START/STOP to begin cooking. 4. When cooking is complete, naturally release the pressure for 10 minutes. Then quick release pressure by turning the pressure release valve to the VENT position. Move slider to AIR FRY/ STOVETOP to unlock the lid, then carefully open it. 5. Use oven mitts to lift the rack and the bowl out of the pot. Use a spoon to press a bean against the side of the pot to make sure it's tender. 6. When the beans are tender, stir in the soy sauce and salt. 7. Taste and adjust the seasonings as needed, then serve the beans with a scoop of brown rice topped with the green onions and coriander. Store leftovers in an airtight container in the fridge for 1 week.

Per Serving: Calories 299; Fat 6.71g; Sodium 600mg; Carbs 53.2g; Fibre 5.2g; Sugar 9.24g; Protein 7.41g

Garlic Black Beans Stew

Prep Time: 15 minutes | Cook Time: 35 minutes | Serves: 6

455 g dried black beans, rinsed and drained
200 g grape or cherry tomatoes
1 large white or yellow onion, chopped
1 head garlic, outer papery skins removed, top third sliced off

and discarded
1 tablespoon chili powder
3 bay leaves
Salt

1. Add the beans, tomatoes, garlic, onion, chili powder, bay, 1 teaspoon salt and 1.2 L water to the pot. Stir to combine, then distribute in an even layer. 2. Close the lid and move the slider to PRESSURE. Make sure the pressure release valve is in the SEAL position. The temperature will default to HIGH, which is the correct setting. Set time to 35 minutes. Select START/ STOP to begin cooking. 3. When cooking is complete, naturally release the pressure for 20 minutes. Then quick release pressure by turning the pressure release valve to the VENT position. Move slider to AIR FRY/ STOVETOP to unlock the lid, then carefully open it. 4. Remove and discard the bay. Using tongs, squeeze the garlic cloves from the head into the beans and stir to combine. Taste and season with salt.

Per Serving: Calories 239; Fat 1.21g; Sodium 237mg; Carbs 44.38g; Fibre 11.2g; Sugar 2.71g; Protein 14.54g

Mushroom, Peas & Barley "Risotto"

Prep Time: 15 minutes | Cook Time: 25 minutes | Serves: 4

1 tablespoon extra-virgin olive oil
1 yellow onion, chopped
200 g cremini mushrooms, chopped
2 cloves garlic, minced
1 teaspoon dried thyme
170 g pearled barley
120 g dried black-eyed peas, unsoaked

480 ml water
1 teaspoon fine sea salt
1 tablespoon soy sauce or tamari
1 generous handful baby spinach
1 tablespoon freshly squeezed lemon juice
25 g grated Parmesan cheese, plus more for serving

1. Add oil to the pot. Move slider to AIR FRY/STOVETOP. Select SEAR/SAUTÉ and set to 3. Select START/STOP to begin cooking. 2. Once the oil is hot, add the onion and mushrooms and sauté until the onion is softened, about 5 minutes. Press START/STOP to end the cooking function and stir in the garlic while the pot is still hot. 3. Stir in the thyme, barley, peas, and water. 4. Close the lid and move the slider to PRESSURE. Make sure the pressure release valve is in the SEAL position. The temperature will default to HIGH, which is the correct setting. Set time to 20 minutes. Select START/STOP to begin cooking. 5. When cooking is complete, naturally release the pressure for 10 minutes. Then quick release pressure by turning the pressure release valve to the VENT position. Move slider to AIR FRY/ STOVETOP to unlock the lid, then carefully open it. 6. Stir in the spinach, salt, soy sauce, lemon juice, and Parmesan until the spinach wilts and the cheese melts. 7. Taste and adjust the seasoning as needed, and serve immediately with additional Parmesan on the side. 8. Store leftovers in an airtight container in the fridge for 5 days.

Per Serving: Calories 447; Fat 7.8g; Sodium 869mg; Carbs 89.09g; Fibre 16.7g; Sugar 3.87g; Protein 15.23g

Wild Rice with Hazelnuts & Apricots

Prep Time: 15 minutes | Cook Time: 5 minutes | Serves: 8

380 g wild rice, rinsed
720 ml vegetable stock
600 ml water
2 teaspoons sea salt

1 tablespoon butter
60 g chopped hazelnuts
60 g chopped dried apricots

1. Place all ingredients into the pot, stir well. 2. Close the lid and move the slider to PRESSURE. Make sure the pressure release valve is in the SEAL position. The temperature will default to HIGH, which is the correct setting. Set time to 30 minutes. Select START/STOP to begin cooking. 3. When cooking is complete, naturally release the pressure for 5 minutes. Then quick release pressure by turning the pressure release valve to the VENT position. Move slider to AIR FRY/ STOVETOP to unlock the lid, then carefully open it. 4. Transfer to a dish and serve warm.

Per Serving: Calories 261; Fat 7.8g; Sodium 810mg; Carbs 41.94g; Fibre 4.9g; Sugar 7.02g; Protein 9.04g

Taco Beans Salad

120 g dried black beans

120 g dried red beans

1 tablespoon avocado oil

1 small onion, peeled and diced

480 ml vegetable stock

½ teaspoon garlic powder

½ teaspoon chili powder

½ teaspoon ground cumin

½ teaspoon sea salt

10 g chopped fresh coriander

75 g mixed greens

1 medium avocado, pitted and sliced

2 large tomatoes, diced

135 g corn kernels

120 g sour cream

24 tortilla chips

1. Rinse and drain beans. 2. Move slider to AIR FRY/STOVETOP. Select SEAR/SAUTÉ and set to 3. Select START/STOP to begin cooking. Heat the oil in the pot. Add onion and sauté 3–5 minutes until onions are translucent. Deglaze the pot by adding stock and scraping the bottom and sides of the pot. Press START/STOP to turn off the SEAR/SAUTÉ function. 3. Stir in the beans, garlic powder, cumin, chili powder, salt, and coriander. 4. Close the lid and move the slider to PRESSURE. Make sure the pressure release valve is in the SEAL position. The temperature will default to HIGH, which is the correct setting. Set time to 30 minutes. Select START/STOP to begin cooking. 5. When cooking is complete, naturally release the pressure for 10 minutes. Then quick release pressure by turning the pressure release valve to the VENT position. Move slider to AIR FRY/ STOVETOP to unlock the lid, then carefully open it. 6. Select SEAR/SAUTÉ and set the heat to Lo1. Simmer the bean mixture unlidded for 10 minutes to thicken. 7. Distribute mixed greens evenly among six bowls. Add a spoonful of beans to each bowl. 8. Garnish with equal amounts of avocado, tomatoes, corn, and sour cream. Top each with 4 tortilla chips and serve.

Per Serving: Calories 332; Fat 13.22g; Sodium 582mg; Carbs 44.93g; Fibre 11.6g; Sugar 5.19g; Protein 12.62g

Tasty Sweet Potato Risotto

4 tablespoons olive oil

4 tablespoons butter, divided

1 medium shallot, peeled and diced

1 medium sweet potato, cut into small chunks

4 cloves garlic, minced

270 g arborio rice

960 ml vegetable stock

½ teaspoon salt

¼ teaspoon black pepper

1. Add oil and 2 tablespoons butter to the pot. Move slider to AIR FRY/STOVETOP. Select SEAR/SAUTÉ and set to 3. Select START/STOP to begin cooking. Once the butter is melted, add shallot and sweet potatoes. Cook, stirring occasionally, 5 minutes. 2. Add garlic and rice and cook for an additional 30 seconds. 3. Pour in stock and deglaze bottom of pot. Press START/STOP to turn off the SEAR/SAUTÉ function. 4. Close the lid and move the slider to PRESSURE. 5. Make sure the pressure release valve is in the SEAL position. The temperature will default to HIGH, which is the correct setting. Set time to 7 minutes. Select START/STOP to begin cooking. 6. When cooking is complete, turn the pressure release valve to the vent position for a quick pressure release. Move slider to the right to unlock the lid, then carefully open it. 7. Mix in remaining 2 tablespoons butter, salt, and pepper. 8. Serve hot.

Per Serving: Calories 485; Fat 36.36g; Sodium 962mg; Carbs 44.81g; Fibre 13.2g; Sugar 6.29g; Protein 11.08g

Chapter 3 Snacks and Starters Recipes

Hoisin Meatballs with Sesame Seeds

Prep Time: 15 minutes | Cook Time: 20 minutes | Serves: 6

240 ml dry red wine

3 tbsp. hoisin sauce

2 tbsp. soy sauce

1 large egg, lightly beaten

4 green onions, chopped

40 g finely chopped onion

10 g minced fresh coriander

2 garlic cloves, minced

½ tsp. salt

½ tsp. pepper

455 g minced beef

455 g minced pork

Sesame seeds

1. Add the wine, hoisin sauce and soy sauce to the pot, stir well. Move slider to AIR FRY/STOVETOP. Select SEAR/SAUTÉ and set to Hi5. Select START/STOP to begin preheating. Bring to a boil. Reduce the heat to Lo1; simmer until liquid is reduced slightly. Press START/STOP to turn off the SEAR/SAUTÉ function. 2. In a big bowl, mix together the next seven ingredients. Add beef and pork; mix lightly but thoroughly. Shape into 4 cm meatballs; place in the pot. 3. Close the lid and move the slider to PRESSURE. Make sure the pressure release valve is in the SEAL position. The temperature will default to HIGH, which is the correct setting. Set time to 10 minutes. Select START/STOP to begin cooking. 4. When cooking is complete, turn the pressure release valve to the vent position for a quick pressure release. Move slider to the right to unlock the lid, then carefully open it. 5. Sprinkle with sesame seeds.

Per Serving: Calories 457; Fat 26.6g; Sodium 517mg; Carbs 8.98g; Fibre 1.4g; Sugar 5.48g; Protein 41.41g

Spicy Dill Deviled Eggs

Prep Time: 15 minutes | Cook Time: 4 minutes | Serves: 6

240 ml cold water

12 large eggs

160 g mayonnaise

4 tsp. dill pickle relish

2 tsp. snipped fresh dill

2 tsp. Dijon mustard

1 tsp. coarsely ground pepper

¼ tsp. garlic powder

⅛ tsp. paprika or cayenne pepper

1. Pour water into the pressure cooker pot. Place the Deluxe Reversible Rack in the lower position in the pot; set eggs on the rack. 2. Close the lid and move the slider to PRESSURE. Make sure the pressure release valve is in the SEAL position. The temperature will default to HIGH, which is the correct setting. Set time to 4 minutes. Select START/STOP to begin cooking. 3. When cooking is complete, naturally release the pressure for 5 minutes. Then quick release pressure by turning the pressure release valve to the VENT position. Move slider to AIR FRY/ STOVETOP to unlock the lid, then carefully open it. Immediately place the eggs in a bowl of ice water to cool. 4. Cut eggs lengthwise in half. Remove yolks, reserving the whites. In a bowl, mash yolks. Stir in all remaining ingredients except paprika. Spoon or pipe into egg whites. 5. Refrigerate, covered, at least 30 minutes before serving. Sprinkle with paprika.

Per Serving: Calories 205; Fat 17.77g; Sodium 271mg; Carbs 4.08g; Fibre 0.7g; Sugar 1.51g; Protein 7.25g

Caribbean Chipotle Pork Sliders with Coleslaw

Prep Time: 15 minutes | Cook Time: 75 minutes | Serves: 20

1 large onion, quartered

1 boneless pork shoulder roast

2 chipotle peppers in adobo sauce, finely chopped

3 tbsp. adobo sauce

80 g honey barbecue sauce

Coleslaw:

180 g red cabbage, finely chopped

1 medium mango, peeled and chopped

75 g pineapple tidbits, drained

25 g chopped fresh coriander

60 ml water

4 garlic cloves, minced

1 Tbsp. ground cumin

1 tsp. salt

¼ tsp. pepper

1 tbsp. lime juice

¼ tsp. salt

⅛ tsp. pepper

20 Hawaiian sweet rolls, split and toasted

1. Place onion in the bottom of the pot. Cut roast in half; place over onion. In a small bowl, mix together the chipotle peppers, barbecue sauce, adobo sauce, water, cumin, garlic, salt and pepper; pour over meat. 2. Close the lid and move the slider to PRESSURE. Make sure the pressure release valve is in the SEAL position. The temperature will default to HIGH, which is the correct setting. Set time to 75 minutes. Select START/STOP to begin cooking. 3. When cooking is complete, naturally release the pressure for 10 minutes. Then quick release pressure by turning the pressure release valve to the VENT position. Move slider to AIR FRY/ STOVETOP to unlock the lid, then carefully open it. 4. Remove roast and let cool slightly. Skim fat from cooking juices. If desired, select SEAR/SAUTÉ setting, and adjust for Hi5 heat. Cook the juices until slightly thickened. 5. Shred pork with two forks. Return pork to pressure cooker; stir to heat through. 6. For the coleslaw, combine the cabbage, pineapple, mango, coriander, lime juice, salt and pepper in a big bowl. Place some pork mixture on each roll bottom; top with 2 tbsp. coleslaw. Replace tops.

Per Serving: Calories 405; Fat 14.48g; Sodium 819mg; Carbs 38.82g; Fibre 2.3g; Sugar 25.55g; Protein 29.51g

Juicy Pulled Pork Sliders

Prep Time: 15 minutes | Cook Time: 50 minutes | Serves: 24

1 boneless pork shoulder roast, halved

2 garlic cloves, minced

½ tsp. lemon-pepper seasoning

1 can unsweetened crushed pineapple, undrained

120 ml orange juice

1 jar mango salsa

24 whole wheat dinner rolls, split

1. Rub the roast with garlic and lemon pepper. Transfer to the pot and top with pineapple and orange juice. 2. Close the lid and move the slider to PRESSURE. Make sure the pressure release valve is in the SEAL position. The temperature will default to HIGH, which is the correct setting. Set time to 50 minutes. Select START/STOP to begin cooking. 3. When cooking is complete, turn the pressure release valve to the vent position for a quick pressure release. Move slider to the right to unlock the lid, then carefully open it. 4. A thermometer inserted in pork should read at least 60°C. 5. Remove the roast and let it cool slightly. Skim the fat from cooking juices. Shred pork with 2 forks. Return pork and cooking juices to the pressure cooker. Stir in salsa; heat through. Serve with rolls.

Per Serving: Calories 545; Fat 5.27g; Sodium 197mg; Carbs 100.97g; Fibre 3.6g; Sugar 87.31g; Protein 25.42g

Sour Cream Deviled Eggs with Olives

Prep Time: 10 minutes | Cook Time: 5 minutes | Serves: 16

8 large eggs

60 g fat-free mayonnaise

60 g reduced-fat sour cream

2 tbsp. soft bread crumbs

1 tbsp. prepared mustard

¼ tsp. salt

Dash white pepper

4 pimiento-stuffed olives, sliced

Paprika, optional

1. Add 240 ml water to the pot and place the bottom layer of the Deluxe Reversible Rack in the lower position in the pot. Place the eggs on the rack. 2. Close the lid and move the slider to PRESSURE. Make sure the pressure release valve is in the SEAL position. The temperature will default to HIGH, which is the correct setting. Set time to 5 minutes. Select START/ STOP to begin cooking. 3. When cooking is complete, naturally release the pressure for 5 minutes. Then quick release pressure by turning the pressure release valve to the VENT position. Move slider to AIR FRY/ STOVETOP to unlock the lid, then carefully open it. 4. Immediately place eggs in a bowl of ice water to cool. Remove shells. 5. Cut eggs lengthwise in half. Remove yolks; refrigerate 8 yolk halves for another use. Set whites aside. 6. Mash the remaining yolks in a small bowl. Stir in sour cream, mayonnaise, bread crumbs, mustard, salt and pepper. Stuff or pipe into egg whites. 7. Garnish with sliced olives. If desired, sprinkle with paprika.

Per Serving: Calories 50; Fat 2.59g; Sodium 97mg; Carbs 4.47g; Fibre 0.4g; Sugar 0.59g; Protein 2.12g

Turkey Cabbage Dumplings

Prep Time: 20 minutes | Cook Time: 7 minutes | Serves: 5

45 g finely shredded Chinese or napa cabbage

2 tbsp. minced fresh coriander

2 tbsp. minced chives

1 large egg, lightly beaten

4 tsp. rice vinegar

2 garlic cloves, minced

1½ tsp. sesame oil

½ tsp. salt

½ tsp. ground ginger

½ tsp. Chinese five-spice powder

¼ tsp. grated lemon zest

¼ tsp. pepper

350 g lean minced turkey

30 pot sticker or gyoza wrappers

9 Chinese or napa cabbage leaves

Sweet chili sauce, optional

1. Mix the first 12 ingredients in a large bowl. Add turkey; mix lightly but thoroughly. 2. Place 1 tbsp. filling in centre of each pot sticker wrapper. Moisten wrapper edge with water. Fold the wrapper over filling; seal edges, pleating the front side several times to form a pleated pouch. 3. Stand dumplings on a work surface to flatten bottoms; curve slightly to form crescent shapes, if desired. 4. Add 240 ml water to the pot. Then place the bottom layer of the Deluxe Reversible Rack in the lower position in the pot. Line the tray with 3 cabbage leaves. Arrange 10 dumplings over cabbage (do not stack). 5. Close the lid and move the slider to PRESSURE. Make sure the pressure release valve is in the SEAL position. The temperature will default to HIGH, which is the correct setting. Set time to 7 minutes. Select START/STOP to begin cooking. 6. When cooking is complete, quick-release pressure. A thermometer inserted in dumpling should read at least 75°C. 7. Transfer dumplings to a serving plate; keep warm. Discard cabbage and cooking juices. Repeat with additional water, remaining cabbage and dumplings. If desired, serve with the chili sauce.

Per Serving: Calories 707; Fat 10.94g; Sodium 1396mg; Carbs 116.55g; Fibre 4.8g; Sugar 2.47g; Protein 33.15g

Parmesan Crab and Courgette Dip

Prep Time: 15 minutes | Cook Time: 13 minutes | Serves: 8

1 medium grated courgette

200 g cream cheese, room temperature

300 g lump crabmeat, drained and picked over for shells

40 g peeled and diced sweet onion

½ teaspoon lemon juice

⅛ teaspoon Worcestershire sauce

2 teaspoons prepared horseradish

¼ teaspoon smoked paprika

¼ teaspoon cayenne pepper

1 teaspoon salt

¼ teaspoon ground black pepper

240 ml water

25 g grated Parmesan cheese

1. Squeeze grated courgette in paper towels to extract excess moisture. 2. Mix together the courgette, crab, cream cheese, onion, lemon juice, Worcestershire sauce, smoked paprika, horseradish, cayenne pepper, salt, and pepper in a medium bowl. Transfer to a oven-safe bowl. 3. Pour water into the pot and place the bottom layer of the Deluxe Reversible Rack in the lower position in the pot. 4. Place the bowl on the rack and close the lid. Move slider to PRESSURE, making sure the pressure release valve is in the SEAL position. The temperature will default to HIGH, which is the correct setting. Set time to 8 minutes. Select START/STOP to begin cooking. 5. When cooking is complete, turn the pressure release valve to the vent position for a quick pressure release. Move slider to the right to unlock the lid, then carefully open it. 6. Sprinkle the Parmesan cheese on top. 7. Move slider to AIR FRY/STOVETOP. Select BROIL. Press START/STOP to begin cooking. Broil for 5 minutes to brown the Parmesan. Serve warm.

Per Serving: Calories 184; Fat 11.93g; Sodium 507mg; Carbs 2.88g; Fibre 0.2g; Sugar 1.88g; Protein 16.88g

Prawns with Thai-Style Sauce

Prep Time: 15 minutes | Cook Time: 1 minute | Serves: 10

Dipping Sauce:

120 g mayonnaise

60 g sour cream

60 g Thai sweet chili sauce

Prawns:

1 (300 ml) bottle gluten-free beer

1 tablespoon sriracha

2 teaspoons lime juice

1.8 kg large uncooked prawns, peeled and deveined

1. In a small bowl, mix the dipping sauce ingredients. Refrigerate covered until ready to serve. 2. Pour beer into the pot and place the Cook & Crisp Basket in the pot. Place prawns in the basket. 3. Close the lid and move the slider to PRESSURE. Make sure the pressure release valve is in the SEAL position. The temperature will default to HIGH, which is the correct setting. Set time to 1 minute. Select START/STOP to begin cooking. 4. When cooking is complete, turn the pressure release valve to the vent position for a quick pressure release. Move slider to the right to unlock the lid, then carefully open it. 5. Transfer the prawns to serving dish and serve warm or cold with dipping sauce.

Per Serving: Calories 253; Fat 10.83g; Sodium 1445mg; Carbs 9.82g; Fibre 1.2g; Sugar 1.92g; Protein 27.25g

Chinese Spiced Chicken Wings

Prep Time: 15 minutes | Cook Time: 16 minutes | Serves: 6

60 ml tamari

60 ml apple cider vinegar

1 teaspoon sriracha

2 teaspoons Chinese five-spice powder

1 tablespoon light brown sugar

3 cloves garlic, peeled and minced

2 tablespoons sesame oil

5 spring onions, sliced and separated into whites and greens

1.3 kg chicken wings, separated at the joint

240 ml water

20 g toasted sesame seeds

1. Combine the tamari, apple cider vinegar, sriracha, Chinese five-spice powder, brown sugar, garlic, sesame oil, and whites of spring onions in a large bowl, stir to mix well. Transfer 2 tablespoons of sauce to a small bowl, set aside. 2. Add chicken wings to sauce in large bowl and toss to coat well. Refrigerate covered at least one hour or up to overnight. 3. Add water to the pot and place the bottom layer of the Deluxe Reversible Rack in the lower position in the pot. Place chicken wings on the rack, arranging them so they aren't sitting on top of one another; place them standing up if necessary. 4. Close the lid and move the slider to PRESSURE. Make sure the pressure release valve is in the SEAL position. The temperature will default to HIGH, which is the correct setting. Set time to 10 minutes. Select START/STOP to begin cooking. 5. When cooking is complete, naturally release the pressure for 10 minutes. Then quick release pressure by turning the pressure release valve to the VENT position. Move slider to AIR FRY/ STOVETOP to unlock the lid, then carefully open it. 6. Brush with 2 tablespoons of reserved sauce. Close the lid and move the slider to the AIR FRY/ STOVETOP. Select BROIL. Broil the chicken wings for 3 minutes on each side to crisp the chicken. 7. Transfer wings to a serving dish and garnish with sesame seeds and greens of spring onions.

Per Serving: Calories 421; Fat 17.76g; Sodium 1597mg; Carbs 8.95g; Fibre 2.2g; Sugar 4.08g; Protein 54.43g

Pickle Deviled Eggs

Prep Time: 15 minutes | Cook Time: 4 minutes | Serves: 6

240 ml water

6 large eggs

3 tablespoons mayonnaise

1 teaspoon yellow mustard

½ teaspoon dill pickle juice

1 teaspoon finely diced dill pickles

⅛ teaspoon smoked paprika

⅛ teaspoon salt

⅛ teaspoon ground black pepper

20 g crushed dill pickle–flavoured potato chips

1. Add water to the pot and place the bottom layer of the Deluxe Reversible Rack in the lower position in the pot. Place eggs on the tray. 2. Close the lid and move the slider to PRESSURE. Make sure the pressure release valve is in the SEAL position. The temperature will default to HIGH, which is the correct setting. Set time to 4 minutes. Select START/STOP to begin cooking. 3. When cooking is complete, turn the pressure release valve to the vent position for a quick pressure release. Move slider to the right to unlock the lid, then carefully open it. 4. Create an ice bath by adding a cup of ice and 240 ml of water to a medium bowl. Transfer eggs to ice bath to stop the cooking process. 5. Peel eggs. Slice each egg in half lengthwise and place yolks in a small bowl. Place egg white halves on a serving tray. 6. Add mayonnaise, mustard, diced pickles, pickle juice, salt, smoked paprika, and pepper to the small bowl with yolks. Use a fork to blend until smooth. 7. Spoon yolk filling into egg white halves. Sprinkle on crushed chips right before serving so they don't get soggy.

Per Serving: Calories 130; Fat 9.77g; Sodium 547mg; Carbs 6.95g; Fibre 1.4g; Sugar 1.49g; Protein 3.7g

Classic Aubergine Dip

Time: 10 minutes | Cook Time: 10 minutes | Serves: 8

1 tablespoon sesame oil
1 large aubergine, peeled and diced
4 cloves garlic, peeled and minced
120 ml water
10 g chopped fresh parsley, divided
¼ teaspoon ground cumin

½ teaspoon salt
2 tablespoons fresh lemon juice
2 tablespoons tahini
1 tablespoon olive oil
¼ teaspoon paprika

1. Add sesame oil to the pot. Move slider to AIR FRY/STOVETOP. Select SEAR/SAUTÉ and set to 3. Select START/STOP to begin cooking. Heat sesame oil in the pot. Add aubergine and sauté for 4-5 minutes until it softens. Add the garlic and cook for an additional minute. Add water. 2. Close the lid and move the slider to PRESSURE. Make sure the pressure release valve is in the SEAL position. The temperature will default to HIGH, which is the correct setting. Set time to 4 minutes. Select START/STOP to begin cooking. 3.When cooking is complete, turn the pressure release valve to the vent position for a quick pressure release. Move slider to the right to unlock the lid, then carefully open it. 4. Strain the cooked aubergine and garlic. Add to a food processor or blender along with half of parsley, lemon juice, cumin, salt, and tahini. Pulse to process. 5. Add the olive oil and process until smooth. Transfer to a serving dish and garnish with remaining chopped parsley and sprinkle with paprika.

Per Serving: Calories 74; Fat 5.58g; Sodium 153mg; Carbs 5.77g; Fibre 2.5g; Sugar 2.57g; Protein 1.49g

Black-Eyed Peas and Corn Dip

Prep Time: 15 minutes | Cook Time: 35 minutes | Serves: 10

2 tablespoons plus 60 ml olive oil, divided
1 large sweet onion, peeled and diced
1 small jalapeño, seeded and diced
2 stalks celery, diced small
3 cloves garlic, minced
455 g dried black-eyed peas
1 slice bacon
480 ml chicken stock

240 ml water
1 small green pepper, seeded and diced
4 small Roma tomatoes, diced (including dicing juice)
240 g corn kernels
½ small red onion, peeled and diced
Juice of 1 lime
1 tablespoon red wine vinegar
10 g chopped fresh coriander

1. Move slider to AIR FRY/STOVETOP. Select SEAR/SAUTÉ and set to 3. Select START/STOP to begin cooking. Heat 1 tablespoon olive oil in the pot. Add onion, jalapeño, and celery and sauté for 3–5 minutes until onions are translucent. Add garlic and heat for 1 more minute. 2. Add another tablespoon of olive oil. Add black-eyed peas and bacon. Toss to combine, then slowly pour in stock and water. 3. Close the lid and move the slider to PRESSURE. Make sure the pressure release valve is in the SEAL position. The temperature will default to HIGH, which is the correct setting. Set time to 30 minutes. Select START/STOP to begin cooking. 4. When cooking is complete, naturally release the pressure for 5 minutes. Then quick release pressure by turning the pressure release valve to the VENT position. Move slider to AIR FRY/ STOVETOP to unlock the lid, then carefully open it. Discard bacon. 5. Using a slotted spoon, transfer bean mixture to a serving dish. Let cool. Add in pepper, tomatoes, red onion, corn, lime juice, 60 ml olive oil, vinegar, and coriander and toss to combine. 6. Refrigerate overnight to marry flavours. Serve warmed or chilled.

Per Serving: Calories 302; Fat 23.49g; Sodium 650mg; Carbs 10.93g; Fibre 1.8g; Sugar 4.03g; Protein 12.49g

Healthy Artichokes

Prep Time: 10 minutes | Cook Time: 5 minutes | Serves: 6

6 medium artichokes

240 ml water

3 cloves garlic, quartered

Juice of 1 lemon

1 teaspoon sea salt

1. Clean artichokes by clipping off the top third of the leaves and removing the tougher exterior leaves. Trim the bottoms so that they have a flat surface to prop up in the pot. 2. Add water, garlic, and lemon juice to the pot. Then place the bottom layer of the Deluxe Reversible Rack in the lower position in the pot. Place artichokes upright on the rack and sprinkle with the salt. 3. Close the lid and move the slider to PRESSURE. Make sure the pressure release valve is in the SEAL position. The temperature will default to HIGH, which is the correct setting. Set time to 5 minutes. Select START/STOP to begin cooking. 4. When cooking is complete, turn the pressure release valve to the vent position for a quick pressure release. Move slider to the right to unlock the lid, then carefully open it. 5. Lift the artichokes very carefully out of the pot (they will be so tender that they may fall apart), transfer to a plate, and serve.

Per Serving: Calories 80; Fat 0.27g; Sodium 541mg; Carbs 18.07g; Fibre 8.8g; Sugar 1.82g; Protein 5.42g

Savoy Beef Stuffed Cabbage Rolls

Prep Time: 15 minutes | Cook Time: 17 minutes | Serves: 6

1 medium head savoy cabbage

720 ml water, divided

225 g minced beef

185 g long-grain rice

1 small red pepper, seeded and minced

1 medium onion, peeled and diced

240 ml beef stock

1 tablespoon olive oil

2 tablespoons minced fresh mint

1 teaspoon dried tarragon

1 teaspoon salt

½ teaspoon ground black pepper

2 tablespoons lemon juice

1. Wash the cabbage. Remove the large outer leaves and set aside. Remove remaining cabbage leaves and place them in the pot. Pour in 240 ml water. 2. Move slider to SteamCrisp and select Steam & Crisp. Cook at 200°C and for 1 minute. 3. Then, move slider to PRESSURE. Make sure the pressure release valve is in the SEAL position. The temperature will default to LOW, which is the correct setting. Set time to 1 minute. Select START/STOP to begin cooking. 4. When cooking is complete, turn the pressure release valve to the vent position for a quick pressure release. Move slider to the right to unlock the lid, then carefully open it. 5. Drain the cabbage leaves in a colander and then move them to a cotton towel. 6. In a medium bowl, combine the beef, rice, onion, pepper, stock, olive oil, tarragon, mint, salt, and pepper. Stir to mix well. 7. Place the reserved (uncooked) cabbage leaves on the bottom of the pot. 8. Remove the stem running down the centre of each steamed cabbage leaf and tear each leaf in half lengthwise. Place 1 tablespoon of the beef mixture in the centre of each cabbage piece. 9. Loosely fold the sides of the leaf over the filling and then fold the top and bottom of the leaf over the folded sides. As you complete them, place each stuffed cabbage leaf in the pot. 10. Pour 480 ml water and the lemon juice over the stuffed cabbage rolls. 11. Close the lid and move the slider to PRESSURE. Make sure the pressure release valve is in the SEAL position. The temperature will default to HIGH, which is the correct setting. Set time to 15 minutes. Select START/STOP to begin cooking. 12. When timer beeps, let pressure release naturally for 10 minutes. Quick-release any additional pressure until float valve drops and then open the lid. 13. Carefully move the stuffed cabbage rolls to a serving platter. Serve warm.

Per Serving: Calories 357; Fat 13.51g; Sodium 525mg; Carbs 45.27g; Fibre 2.8g; Sugar 16.54g; Protein 13.49g

Chapter 4 Vegetables and Sides Recipes

Sour Cream Cabbage

Prep Time: 15 minutes | Cook Time: 5 minutes | Serves: 6

240 ml water

1 medium-large green or savoy cabbage, sliced

55 g grass-fed butter

115 g sour cream

¾ tsp sea salt

114 g precooked crispy bacon or turkey bacon, crumbled, for garnish (optional)

1. Pour the water into the pot and place the bottom layer of the Deluxe Reversible Rack in the lower position in the pot. Layer the sliced cabbage on the rack. 2. Close the lid and move the slider to PRESSURE. Make sure the pressure release valve is in the SEAL position. The temperature will default to HIGH, which is the correct setting. Set time to 2 minutes. Select START/STOP to begin cooking. 3. Once the timer beeps, press START/STOP. Quick release pressure by turning the pressure release valve to the VENT position. Move slider to the right to unlock the lid, then carefully open it. 4. Carefully remove the cabbage and the rack, setting the cabbage aside. Pour out and discard the water that remains in the pot. 5. Place the butter in the pot and select SEAR/SAUTÉ and set to 3. Press START/STOP to begin cooking. Once the butter has melted, return the cabbage to the pot and sauté for 1 minute, stirring occasionally. Add the sour cream and salt and sauté for 2 minutes, stirring occasionally. Press START/STOP to turn off the SEAR/SAUTÉ function. 6. Serve immediately, garnished with the crumbled crispy bacon (if using).

Per Serving: Calories 196; Fat 15.51g; Sodium 623mg; Carbs 12.87g; Fibre 3.4g; Sugar 5.4g; Protein 4.77g

Herbed Carrots & Parsnips

Prep Time: 15 minutes | Cook Time: 8 minutes | Serves: 6

240 ml water

4 large carrots, peeled and thickly sliced on the diagonal

3 medium parsnips, peeled and sliced on the diagonal

45 g grass-fed butter or ghee

2 cloves garlic, minced

1 tsp sea salt

1 tsp dried thyme

1 tsp dried dill

1. Pour the water into the pot and place the bottom layer of the Deluxe Reversible Rack in the lower position in the pot. Layer the carrots and parsnips in the on the rack. 2. Close the lid and move the slider to PRESSURE. Make sure the pressure release valve is in the SEAL position. The temperature will default to HIGH, which is the correct setting. Set time to 3 minutes. Select START/STOP to begin cooking. 3. When cooking is complete, turn the pressure release valve to the vent position for a quick pressure release. Move slider to the right to unlock the lid, then carefully open it. 4. Carefully remove the carrots and parsnips and the rack, setting the carrots and parsnips aside. Pour out and discard the water that remains in the pot. 5. Place your healthy fat of choice in the pot and press SEAR/SAUTÉ and set to 3. Press START/STOP to begin cooking. Once the fat has melted, add the garlic and sauté for 1 minute, stirring occasionally. 6. Add the carrots and parsnips back to the pot along with the salt, thyme and dill. Give everything a stir, then sauté for 3 minutes, stirring occasionally. Press START/STOP. Serve immediately.

Per Serving: Calories 104; Fat 6.02g; Sodium 397mg; Carbs 12.72g; Fibre 3.4g; Sugar 3.3g; Protein 1g

Thyme Celery Root–Cauliflower Mash with Caramelized Onion

Prep Time: 15 minutes | Cook Time: 13 minutes | Serves: 8

6 tbsp (85 g) grass-fed butter or ghee, divided

1 yellow onion, sliced

¾ tsp sea salt, divided

240 ml water

4 small celery roots, peeled and cut into large cubes

1 small head cauliflower, cut into florets

2 small parsnips, peeled and cut into large cubes

2 tbsp (30 ml) chicken or vegetable stock, or bone stock

Leaves from 2 sprigs thyme

½ tsp garlic granules or powder

1. Place 2 tablespoons (28 g) of your healthy fat of choice in the pot. Move slider to AIR FRY/STOVETOP. Select SEAR/SAUTÉ and set to 3. Select START/STOP to begin cooking. 2. Once the fat has melted, add the onion and ¼ teaspoon of the salt and sauté, stirring occasionally, for about 7 minutes, or until the onion is light golden brown and caramelized. Press START/STOP, transfer the caramelized onion to a bowl or plate, set aside. 3. Pour the water into the pot and place the bottom layer of the Deluxe Reversible Rack in the lower position in the pot. Layer the celery roots, cauliflower and parsnips on the rack. 4. Close the lid and move the slider to PRESSURE. Make sure the pressure release valve is in the SEAL position. The temperature will default to HIGH, which is the correct setting. Set time to 5 minutes. Select START/STOP to begin cooking. 5. When cooking is complete, naturally release the pressure for 10 minutes. Then quick release pressure by turning the pressure release valve to the VENT position. Move slider to AIR FRY/ STOVETOP to unlock the lid, then carefully open it. 6. Using a large slotted spoon, carefully remove the vegetables and place them in a blender or food processor. Add the remaining 4 tablespoons (57 g) of your healthy fat of choice plus the stock, thyme, remaining ½ teaspoon of salt and the garlic granules. Pulse or blend for 30 seconds to 1 minute, or until completely smooth. 7. Serve the mash immediately, topped with the reserved caramelised onions.

Per Serving: Calories 108; Fat 9.43g; Sodium 244mg; Carbs 5.6g; Fibre 1.7g; Sugar 1.85g; Protein 1.16g

Lemon-Garlic Smashed Red Potatoes

Prep Time: 15 minutes | Cook Time: 11 minutes | Serves: 4

680 g baby red potatoes

240 ml water

2 tbsp (30 ml) avocado oil or extra-virgin olive oil

3 cloves garlic, minced

½ tsp sea salt, plus more to taste

½ tsp freshly ground black pepper

2 tbsp (30 ml) fresh lemon juice

1. Wash and dry the potatoes. Pour the water into the pot and place the bottom layer of the Deluxe Reversible Rack in the lower position in the pot. Place the potatoes on the rack. 2. Close the lid and move the slider to PRESSURE. Make sure the pressure release valve is in the SEAL position. The temperature will default to HIGH, which is the correct setting. Set time to 6 minutes. Select START/STOP to begin cooking. 3. When cooking is complete, turn the pressure release valve to the vent position for a quick pressure release. Move slider to the right to unlock the lid, then carefully open it. 4. Remove the potatoes and place on a large baking sheet. Using a glass or the back of a spoon, gently press down on the potatoes, or smash them. 5. Combine the oil and garlic in a small bowl. Brush over each of the potatoes, then sprinkle with salt and pepper. 6. Place the potatoes on the rack in the pot. Move slider to AIR FRY/STOVETOP. Select BROIL. Broil for 4 to 5 minutes, or until crispy. 7. Remove from the oven and drizzle with the lemon juice. Sprinkle with additional salt to taste. Serve hot.

Per Serving: Calories 185; Fat 7.08g; Sodium 323mg; Carbs 28.56g; Fibre 3.1g; Sugar 2.41g; Protein 3.42g

Cheese Corned Beef & Cabbage Slaw

Prep Time: 15 minutes | Cook Time: 85 minutes | Serves: 6

237 ml beef stock
1.4 kg corned beef
295 g mayonnaise
10 ml cider vinegar

¼ tsp celery seeds
1 small head green cabbage, sliced thinly, core removed
110 g diced Swiss cheese

1. Combine the beef stock and the corned beef along with the contents of its seasoning packet in the pot. 2. Close the lid and move the slider to PRESSURE. Make sure the pressure release valve is in the SEAL position. The temperature will default to HIGH, which is the correct setting. Set time to 85 minutes. Select START/STOP to begin cooking. 3. When cooking is complete, turn the pressure release valve to the vent position for a quick pressure release. Move slider to the right to unlock the lid, then carefully open it. Transfer the corned beef to a cutting board to cool. 4. In the meantime, mix together the mayonnaise, vinegar and celery seeds in a small bowl. Chop the corned beef into bite-size pieces. In a big bowl, combine the beef, mayonnaise mixture, cabbage and cheese and stir well. 5. Refrigerate for at least 1 hour before serving.
Per Serving: Calories 553; Fat 35.06g; Sodium 683mg; Carbs 3.37g; Fibre 0.6g; Sugar 1g; Protein 56.27g

Red Wine Braised Mushroom

Prep Time: 15 minutes | Cook Time: 35 minutes | Serves: 6

2 tbsp (30 ml) extra-virgin olive oil
2 tbsp (28 g) unsalted butter
455 g whole white mushrooms, cut in half
1 yellow onion, diced
2 carrots, peeled and sliced
1 celery rib, diced
Salt
Freshly ground black pepper
½ tsp dried thyme

1 clove garlic, grated
1 tbsp (15 ml) balsamic vinegar
240 ml dry red wine
240 ml water
175 ml beef or vegetable stock, divided
30 g dried shiitake mushrooms
1 tbsp (8 g) cornflour
2 tbsp (32 g) tomato paste

1. Move slider to AIR FRY/STOVETOP. Select SEAR/SAUTÉ and set to 3. Select START/STOP to begin preheating. Allow unit to preheat for 5 minutes. After 5 minutes, add the oil and butter. When the butter melts, add the white mushrooms. Cook for 15 minutes, or until the mushrooms are golden. 2. Add the onion, carrots, celery, thyme, salt and pepper, and garlic. Sauté for 3 minutes. Press START/STOP, then mix in the red wine, vinegar, water, 115 ml of the stock and the dried mushrooms. 3. Close the lid and move the slider to PRESSURE. Make sure the pressure release valve is in the SEAL position. The temperature will default to HIGH, which is the correct setting. Set time to 9 minutes. Select START/STOP to begin cooking. 4. When cooking is complete, turn the pressure release valve to the vent position for a quick pressure release. Move slider to the right to unlock the lid, then carefully open it. 5. In a bowl, whisk together the cornflour and remaining 60 ml of stock. 6. Stir the cornflour slurry into the pot along with the tomato paste. Adjust the salt and pepper to taste.
Per Serving: Calories 116; Fat 5.67g; Sodium 395mg; Carbs 11.24g; Fibre 2.9g; Sugar 4.48g; Protein 4.83g

Buttered Mashed Potatoes

Prep Time: 10 minutes | Cook Time: 8 minutes | Serves: 2

455 g Russet potatoes, peeled and quartered

2 garlic cloves, minced

1 teaspoon Salt

55 g butter

60 ml milk

60 g cream cheese (optional)

Freshly ground black pepper

Fresh chives, chopped (optional)

1. Put the potatoes in the pot, add the garlic, and season with salt. Cover the potatoes with water. 2. Close the lid and move the slider to PRESSURE. Make sure the pressure release valve is in the SEAL position. The temperature will default to HIGH, which is the correct setting. Set time to 8 minutes. Select START/STOP to begin cooking. 3. Quick release the pressure at the end of the cook time. Carefully remove the pot from the cooker, drain the water through a large sieve or colander over a big bowl, reserve the cooking liquid, set aside. 4. Return the potatoes to the pot and mash them using a potato masher or the back of a wooden spoon. Add in the butter, milk, and cream cheese (if using) and stir to mix well. Add some of the reserved potato water, if needed, to get the desired creaminess. Season with salt and pepper. 5. Serve topped with chives (if desired).

Per Serving: Calories 496; Fat 32.83g; Sodium 1322mg; Carbs 44.9g; Fibre 3.2g; Sugar 4.06g; Protein 8.46g

Potato Yogurt Salad

Prep Time: 15 minutes | Cook Time: 4 minutes | Serves: 2

4 medium Russet potatoes, peeled and cubed

2 eggs

1 celery stalk, chopped

¼ red onion, chopped

60 g plain Greek yogurt

2 tablespoons yellow mustard

Salt

Freshly ground black pepper

Paprika, for garnish

1. Put 240 ml and the potatoes into the pot. Put the whole eggs (in their shells) on top of the potatoes. 2. Close the lid and move the slider to PRESSURE. Make sure the pressure release valve is in the SEAL position. The temperature will default to HIGH, which is the correct setting. Set time to 4 minutes. Select START/STOP to begin cooking. 3. Use a quick release at the end of the cook time. Open the lid and take out the eggs. Carefully remove the cooker pot, then drain the potatoes through a large sieve or colander and set aside. 4. Rinse the eggs under cold water until they are no longer steaming. Place them into a bowl of cold water to chill. When cooled, peel and roughly chop them. 5. Mix together the potatoes, eggs, onion, celery, yogurt, and mustard in a medium bowl, then season with salt and pepper. 6. Transfer the potato salad to a serving bowl, sprinkle with paprika, and cover and refrigerate until ready to serve.

Per Serving: Calories 743; Fat 10.94g; Sodium 442mg; Carbs 138.02g; Fibre 10.9g; Sugar 6.78g; Protein 27.7g

Pecans & Marshmallows Loaded Sweet Potatoes

Prep Time: 15 minutes | Cook Time: 20 minutes | Serves: 2

2 medium sweet potatoes
4 tablespoons butter, at room temperature
2 teaspoons ground cinnamon

60 g packed brown sugar
30 g chopped pecans
85 g mini marshmallows

1. Place the bottom layer of the Deluxe Reversible Rack in the lower position in the pot. and add 240 ml. 2. Place the sweet potatoes on the rack inside the pot. 3. Close the lid and move the slider to PRESSURE. Make sure the pressure release valve is in the SEAL position. The temperature will default to HIGH, which is the correct setting. Set time to 15 minutes. Select START/STOP to begin cooking. 4. When cooking is complete, naturally release the pressure for 10 minutes. Then quick release pressure by turning the pressure release valve to the VENT position. Move slider to AIR FRY/ STOVETOP to unlock the lid, then carefully open it. 5. Put the butter in a small bowl. Sprinkle on the cinnamon and mix together until fully combined. 6. Transfer the potatoes to a clean work surface and let cool a bit. Cut both potatoes open, mash the flesh a bit, and divide the butter mixture between them. Sprinkle with the brown sugar, pecans, and marshmallows. 7. Put the potatoes in a baking dish that fits the pot and place on the rack. Close the lid and move the slider to AIR FRY/STOVETOP. Select BROIL. Select START/STOP to begin cooking. Broil for 3 to 4 minutes, or until the marshmallows are lightly browned. Serve hot.
Per Serving: Calories 541; Fat 32.93g; Sodium 236mg; Carbs 62.82g; Fibre 6.5g; Sugar 39.82g; Protein 3.75g

Lime Cauliflower Rice with Coriander

Prep Time: 15 minutes | Cook Time: 5 minutes | Serves: 2

1 medium to large head cauliflower, broken into florets
2 tablespoons olive oil
¼ teaspoon Salt

30 g chopped fresh coriander
Juice of 1 lime

1. Add 240 ml to the pot and place the bottom layer of the Deluxe Reversible Rack in the lower position in the pot. Put the cauliflower florets on the rack. 2. Close the lid and move the slider to PRESSURE. Make sure the pressure release valve is in the SEAL position. The temperature will default to HIGH, which is the correct setting. Set time to 1 minute. Select START/ STOP to begin cooking. 3. When cooking is complete, turn the pressure release valve to the vent position for a quick pressure release. Move slider to the right to unlock the lid, then carefully open it. 4. Transfer the cauliflower to a plate. Carefully drain the water from the pot, wipe the pot dry, and put it back in the cooker. 5. Move slider to AIR FRY/STOVETOP. Select SEAR/ SAUTÉ and set to Lo1. Select START/STOP to begin cooking. Heat the olive oil in the pot. Add the cooked cauliflower and break it up with a potato masher. 6. Season with the salt, add the coriander, and stir gently while the cauliflower rice heats. Add the lime juice and stir. Serve.
Per Serving: Calories 160; Fat 13.93g; Sodium 335mg; Carbs 8.73g; Fibre 3g; Sugar 2.97g; Protein 2.81g

Courgette and Tomato Bowls

Prep Time: 10 minutes | Cook Time: 12 minutes | Serves: 4

1 tablespoon avocado oil

1 large onion, peeled and diced

3 cloves garlic, minced

1 can diced tomatoes, including juice

120 ml water

1 tablespoon Italian seasoning

1 teaspoon sea salt

½ teaspoon ground black pepper

2 medium courgette, spiraled

1. Add avocado oil to the pot. Move slider to AIR FRY/STOVETOP. Select SEAR/SAUTÉ and set to Lo1. Select START/STOP to begin cooking. Once the oil is hot, add onions and sauté for 3–5 minutes until translucent. Add garlic and cook for one minute. Add tomatoes, Italian seasoning, water, salt, and pepper. Add courgette and toss to combine. Press START/STOP. 2. Close the lid and move the slider to PRESSURE. Make sure the pressure release valve is in the SEAL position. The temperature will default to HIGH, which is the correct setting. Set time to 1 minute. Select START/STOP to begin cooking. 3. When cooking is complete, naturally release the pressure for 5 minutes. Then quick release pressure by turning the pressure release valve to the VENT position. Move slider to AIR FRY/ STOVETOP to unlock the lid, then carefully open it. 4. Transfer courgette to four bowls. Select SEAR/SAUTÉ and set to Lo1, and simmer sauce in the pot unlidded for 5 minutes. Ladle over courgette and serve immediately.

Per Serving: Calories 93; Fat 4.11g; Sodium 981mg; Carbs 13.48g; Fibre 5.1g; Sugar 7.49g; Protein 2.57g

Asian Mushroom & Sweet Potato Bowls

Prep Time: 35 minutes | Cook Time: 3 minutes | Serves: 4

2 tablespoons coconut aminos

1 tablespoon white vinegar

2 teaspoons olive oil

1 teaspoon sesame oil

1 tablespoon honey

¼ teaspoon red pepper flakes

3 cloves garlic, minced

1 large sweet potato, peeled and spiraled

455 g shiitake mushrooms, sliced

240 ml vegetable stock

10 g chopped fresh parsley

1. In a big bowl, mix together the coconut aminos, vinegar, sesame oil, olive oil, honey, red pepper flakes, and garlic. 2. Toss sweet potato and shiitake mushrooms in sauce. Cover and refrigerate for 30 minutes. 3. Pour vegetable stock into the pot. Then place the Cook & Crisp Basket in the lower position in the pot. 4. Place the sweet potato mixture on the basket. 5. Close the lid and move the slider to PRESSURE. Make sure the pressure release valve is in the SEAL position. The temperature will default to HIGH, which is the correct setting. Set time to 3 minutes. Select START/STOP to begin cooking. 6. When cooking is complete, naturally release the pressure for 5 minutes. Then quick release pressure by turning the pressure release valve to the VENT position. Move slider to AIR FRY/ STOVETOP to unlock the lid, then carefully open it. 7. Remove basket from the pot and distribute sweet potatoes and mushrooms evenly among four bowls; pour liquid from the pot over bowls and garnish with chopped parsley.

Per Serving: Calories 180; Fat 4.26g; Sodium 173mg; Carbs 35.18g; Fibre 4.9g; Sugar 12.86g; Protein 4.12g

Cheese Potato Onion Pie

Prep Time: 15 minutes | Cook Time: 20 minutes | Serves: 4

360 ml water

2 tbsp butter

680 g potato, peeled and thinly sliced

455 g onions, finely sliced

110 g cheddar cheese, grated

Salt and ground black pepper to taste

2 tbsp chives, chopped

Salad, optional

1. Pour the water into the pot and place the bottom layer of the Deluxe Reversible Rack in the lower position in the pot. 2. Butter baking pan and start by putting the bottom layer of potatoes. 3. Then layer the onion above the potatoes and the cheese; then place a layer of potatoes on top and sprinkle with cheese. Sprinkle with salt and pepper. 4. Cover the pan tightly with aluminum foil and place on the rack. 5. Close the lid and move the slider to PRESSURE. Make sure the pressure release valve is in the SEAL position. The temperature will default to HIGH, which is the correct setting. Set time to 20 minutes. Select START/STOP to begin cooking. 6. Once timer goes off, use a Quick Release. Carefully open the lid. 7. Top with chives and serve with salad.

Per Serving: Calories 347; Fat 15.61g; Sodium 245mg; Carbs 41.82g; Fibre 5.9g; Sugar 6.82g; Protein 11.81g

Delicious Ranch Potatoes

Prep Time: 10 minutes | Cook Time: 10 minutes | Serves: 4

2 tbsp butter

3 large yellow potatoes, cubed

2 tbsp Ranch dressing or seasoning mix

120 ml water

Salt and ground black pepper to taste

1. Move slider to AIR FRY/STOVETOP. Select SEAR/SAUTÉ and set to Lo1. Select START/STOP to begin preheating. Allow unit to preheat for 5 minutes. After 5 minutes, add the butter and melt it. 2. Add the potatoes and stir well. 3. Sprinkle with Ranch seasoning and stir. Add the water to the pot. Press START/STOP to turn off the SEAR/SAUTÉ function. 4. Close the lid and move the slider to PRESSURE. Make sure the pressure release valve is in the SEAL position. The temperature will default to HIGH, which is the correct setting. Set time to 6 minutes. Select START/STOP to begin cooking. 5. When the timer beeps, use a Quick Release. Carefully open the lid. 6. Season with salt and pepper and serve.

Per Serving: Calories 282; Fat 6.03g; Sodium 372mg; Carbs 51.9g; Fibre 6.8g; Sugar 3.2g; Protein 6.07g

Herbed Veggie & Bread Casserole

Prep Time: 15 minutes | Cook Time: 35 minutes | Serves: 8

1 (455-g) loaf gluten-free sourdough bread, cubed

6 tbsp (85 g) grass-fed butter, ghee or avocado oil, plus more for casserole dish

1 small yellow onion, diced

2 celery ribs, diced

1 small fennel bulb, diced

50 g cauliflower rice

2 cloves garlic, finely chopped

1 small sweet apple, cored, peeled and diced (I like Fuji, Gala or Honey crisp apples)

30 g dried cranberries or raisins (optional)

1 tbsp (3 g) chopped fresh sage

1 tbsp (2 g) chopped fresh thyme

1 tbsp (4 g) chopped fresh flat-leaf parsley

1¼ tsp (8 g) sea salt

240 ml chicken or vegetable stock, or bone stock

240 ml water

1. Toast the bread cubes: You can do this on a dry baking sheet in a 180°C oven for 25 minutes. Transfer the toasted bread cubes to a large bowl and set aside. 2. Use your healthy fat of choice to grease a 1.5-L casserole dish that fits inside the pot. Set it aside. 3. Place your healthy fat of choice in the pot. Move slider to AIR FRY/STOVETOP. Select SEAR/SAUTÉ and set to 3. Select START/STOP to begin cooking. Once the fat has melted, add the onion and sauté, stirring occasionally, for 7 minutes, or until light golden brown. Add the celery and fennel and sauté, stirring occasionally, for 3 minutes. Add the cauliflower and garlic and sauté, stirring often, for 2 minutes. Add the apple, dried fruit (if using), parsley, sage, thyme, and salt, stirring to combine. Press START/STOP. 4. Carefully transfer the vegetable mixture and stock into the bowl that contains the toasted bread cubes and gently stir to combine for about 30 seconds, allowing some of the stock to absorb into the bread. 5. Pour the stuffing mixture into the prepared casserole dish, patting down as needed. Cover the casserole dish with its glass lid. If your casserole dish doesn't have a glass lid, you can cover the top of the dish with unbleached parchment paper, then top it with foil and secure it around the edges. 6. Pour the water into the pot and place the Deluxe Reversible Rack in the lower position in the pot. 7. Carefully set the covered casserole dish on top of the rack. 8. Close the lid and move the slider to PRESSURE. Make sure the pressure release valve is in the SEAL position. The temperature will default to HIGH, which is the correct setting. Set time to 23 minutes. Select START/STOP to begin cooking. 9. When cooking is complete, turn the pressure release valve to the vent position for a quick pressure release. Move slider to the right to unlock the lid, then carefully open it. 10. Using an oven mitt, carefully remove the casserole dish and place on a wire rack. Carefully remove the hot lid without dripping any condensation onto the stuffing. 11. Allow the stuffing to cool on a wire rack at room temperature for 20 minutes before serving.

Per Serving: Calories 153; Fat 10.75g; Sodium 571mg; Carbs 13.86g; Fibre 3.6g; Sugar 5.4g; Protein 3.68g

Chapter 5 Soup, Stock and Stock Recipes

Basic Cream Soup

4 tablespoons unsalted butter

2 stalks celery, diced

½ medium yellow onion, peeled and diced

30 g plain flour

½ teaspoon salt

960 ml chicken stock

120 g heavy whipping cream

1. Move slider to AIR FRY/STOVETOP. Select SEAR/SAUTÉ and set to Lo1. Select START/STOP to begin cooking. Melt butter in the pot. Add celery and onion. Sauté until soft, about 8 minutes. Add the flour and salt and cook for one minute. Press the START/STOP button. 2. Whisk in stock slowly. Close the lid and move the slider to PRESSURE. Make sure the pressure release valve is in the SEAL position. The temperature will default to HIGH, which is the correct setting. Set time to 1 minute. Select START/STOP to begin cooking. 3. When the timer beeps, quick-release the pressure. Open lid, press the START/STOP button, then select the SEAR/SAUTÉ button and set to 3. Cook, whisking frequently, until the desired thickness is achieved. Stir in cream. Use immediately.

Per Serving: Calories 86; Fat 6.95g; Sodium 616mg; Carbs 4.51g; Fibre 0.3g; Sugar 1.1g; Protein 1.69g

Classic Beef Stock

1 tablespoon olive oil

455 g chuck or round beef, cut into 8 cm pieces

1 teaspoon sea salt

2 stalks celery, cut into 6cm pieces

1 medium white onion, peeled and quartered

1 medium carrot, peeled and cut into 6 cm pieces

4 cloves garlic, peeled and crushed

1 tablespoon tomato paste

2 sprigs fresh thyme or ½ teaspoon dried thyme

2 sprigs fresh oregano or ½ teaspoon dried oregano

1 teaspoon (about 10) whole black peppercorns

2 L water

1. Move slider to AIR FRY/STOVETOP. Select SEAR/SAUTÉ and set to 3. Select START/STOP to begin cooking. Heat oil in the pot. Add in beef and season with salt and brown on all sides, about 5 minutes per side. Press the START/STOP button. 2. Add celery, onion, carrot, tomato paste, garlic, peppercorns, thyme, oregano, and water to pot and stir well. 3. Close the lid and move the slider to PRESSURE. Make sure the pressure release valve is in the SEAL position. The temperature will default to HIGH, which is the correct setting. Set time to 60 minutes. Select START/STOP to begin cooking. 4. When cooking is complete, naturally release the pressure for 30 minutes. Then quick release pressure by turning the pressure release valve to the VENT position. Move slider to AIR FRY/ STOVETOP to unlock the lid, then carefully open it. 5. Carefully lift out beef and reserve for another use. Strain stock into a jar and use immediately, refrigerate the leftover for up to seven days or freeze for up to three months.

Per Serving: Calories 109; Fat 5.31g; Sodium 351mg; Carbs 3.38g; Fibre 0.8g; Sugar 1.31g; Protein 12.22g

Turkey Celery Stock

Prep Time: 15 minutes | Cook Time: 40 minutes | Serves: 8

1 carcass from a 5.5 kg turkey, broken into pieces

3 stalks celery, chopped

20 g celery leaves

1 medium yellow onion, peeled and quartered

1 medium carrot, chopped

2 cloves garlic, peeled and crushed

2 bay leaves

10 whole black peppercorns

1 sprig fresh sage

1. Place all ingredients in the pot, then fill pot with water to the Max Fill line. 2. Close the lid and move the slider to PRESSURE. Make sure the pressure release valve is in the SEAL position. The temperature will default to HIGH, which is the correct setting. Set time to 40 minutes. Select START/STOP to begin cooking. 3. When cooking is complete, naturally release the pressure for 30 minutes. Then quick release pressure by turning the pressure release valve to the VENT position. Move slider to AIR FRY/ STOVETOP to unlock the lid, then carefully open it. 4. Strain stock into a jar and use immediately, refrigerate for up to seven days, or freeze for up to three months.

Per Serving: Calories 288; Fat 25.34g; Sodium 41mg; Carbs 3.36g; Fibre 1g; Sugar 1.13g; Protein 11.25g

Thyme Beef Stock

Prep Time: 15 minutes | Cook Time: 2½ hours | Serves: 8

2.3 kg beef bones

2 tablespoons olive oil, divided

2 stalks celery, chopped

1 medium white onion, peeled and quartered

1 medium carrot, peeled and cut into 6 cm pieces

120 ml water

2 cloves garlic, peeled and crushed

2 sprigs fresh thyme or ½ teaspoon dried thyme

1 sprig fresh flat-leaf parsley

1 tablespoon tomato paste

1. Move slider to AIR FRY/STOVETOP. Select BAKE/ROAST, setting temperature to 200°C, and setting time to 5 minutes. Select START/STOP to begin preheating. 2. While unit is preheating, toss beef bones in 1 tablespoon oil and arrange on a large rimmed baking sheet that fits the pot. In a big bowl, toss celery, carrot and onion with remaining 1 tablespoon oil and set aside. 3. Place the Deluxe Reversible Rack in the lower position in the pot. Then place the baking sheet with beef bones on the rack. 4. Roast bones for 30 minutes. Turn bones over, and add vegetable mixture to the baking sheet and roast for 30 minutes more until bones are browned and vegetables are soft. Watch bones carefully to avoid scorching. Remove the baking sheet and rack from the pot. 5. Transfer bones and vegetables to the pot. Pour water onto baking sheet and scrape up browned bits. Pour into the pot. 6. Add garlic, parsley, thyme, and tomato paste to the pot, then cover with water to the Max Fill line. Close the lid and move the slider to PRESSURE. Make sure the pressure release valve is in the SEAL position. Set the temperature to LOW and set time to 2 hours. Select START/STOP to begin cooking. 7. When the timer beeps, let pressure release naturally, about 30 minutes. Open the lid. Strain stock into a jar and use immediately, refrigerate for up to seven days, or freeze for up to three months.

Per Serving: Calories 644; Fat 32.85g; Sodium 201mg; Carbs 2.93g; Fibre 0.7g; Sugar 1.26g; Protein 79.4g

Curried Red Lentil Soup

Prep Time: 10 minutes | Cook Time: 20 minutes | Serves: 6

2 tablespoons salted butter

1 medium white onion, peeled and chopped

1 tablespoon red curry paste

½ teaspoon garam masala

½ teaspoon turmeric

½ teaspoon brown sugar

2 cloves garlic, minced

2 teaspoons grated fresh ginger

3 tablespoons tomato paste

180 g red lentils

960 ml chicken stock or vegetable stock

120 ml full-fat canned coconut milk, shaken well

1. Move slider to AIR FRY/STOVETOP. Select SEAR/SAUTÉ and set to 3. Select START/STOP to begin cooking. Melt butter in the pot. Add the onion and cook until tender, about 3 minutes. 2. Add curry paste, garam masala, garlic, brown sugar, turmeric, and ginger and cook until fragrant, about 30 seconds. Stir in tomato paste and cook for 30 seconds. Press the START/STOP button. 3. Add lentils and stock, close lid and move slider to PRESSURE. Make sure the pressure release valve is in the SEAL position. The temperature will default to HIGH, which is the correct setting. Set time to 15 minutes. Select START/STOP to begin cooking. 4. When the timer beeps, let pressure release naturally, about 15 minutes. Open the lid and stir in coconut milk. Serve warm.

Per Serving: Calories 299; Fat 12.84g; Sodium 362mg; Carbs 36.21g; Fibre 6.3g; Sugar 6.64g; Protein 12.72g

Savoury Beef and Lentil Soup

Prep Time: 15 minutes | Cook Time: 40 minutes | Serves: 6

2 tablespoons olive oil

455 g beef stew meat

2 stalks celery, chopped

1 medium onion, chopped

1 medium carrot, chopped

2 cloves garlic, minced

½ teaspoon salt

375 g red lentils

1 large sweet potato, peeled and diced

480 ml chicken stock

1. Move slider to AIR FRY/STOVETOP. Select SEAR/SAUTÉ and set to 3. Select START/STOP to begin cooking. Heat oil in the pot. Add beef and cook, stirring frequently, until well browned, about 10 minutes. 2. Add onion, celery, and carrot and cook until just tender, about 3 minutes. Add the garlic and salt and cook until fragrant, about 30 seconds. Press the START/STOP button. 3. Add lentils, sweet potato, and stock. Close the lid and move the slider to PRESSURE. Make sure the pressure release valve is in the SEAL position. The temperature will default to HIGH, which is the correct setting. Set time to 25 minutes. Select START/STOP to begin cooking. 4. When the timer beeps, let pressure release naturally, about 15 minutes. Open the lid and stir. Serve warm.

Per Serving: Calories 432; Fat 9.97g; Sodium 397mg; Carbs 52.76g; Fibre 8.6g; Sugar 4.55g; Protein 34.88g

Tomato and Beans Soup

Prep Time: 15 minutes | Cook Time: 37 minutes | Serves: 4

1 tablespoon vegetable oil

1 medium white onion, peeled and chopped

2 cloves garlic, minced

1 pound tomatoes, chopped

½ teaspoon dried sage

½ teaspoon black pepper

220 g cannellini beans, soaked overnight and drained

960 ml vegetable stock

1 teaspoon salt

1. Move slider to AIR FRY/STOVETOP. Select SEAR/SAUTÉ and set to 3. Select START/STOP to begin cooking. Heat oil in the pot. Add onion and cook until tender, about 5 minutes. Add garlic and cook until fragrant, about 1 minute. Add tomatoes and cook for one minute. 2. Press the START/STOP button and add sage, beans, pepper, and stock. 3. Close the lid and move the slider to PRESSURE. Make sure the pressure release valve is in the SEAL position. The temperature will default to HIGH, which is the correct setting. Set time to 30 minutes. Select START/STOP to begin cooking. 4. When the timer beeps, let pressure release naturally. Open the lid, stir well, and season with salt. Serve hot.

Per Serving: Calories 162; Fat 5.9g; Sodium 1156mg; Carbs 24.03g; Fibre 5.5g; Sugar 7.95g; Protein 6.13g

Green Split Pea & Ham Soup

Prep Time: 15 minutes | Cook Time: 35 minutes | Serves: 4

1 tablespoon bacon grease

1 large sweet onion, peeled and diced

2 celery stalks, sliced

2 large carrots, peeled and diced

210 g dried green split peas, rinsed

1.2 L chicken stock

1 teaspoon dried oregano

1 pound smoked ham hock

½ teaspoon sea salt

½ teaspoon ground black pepper

4 tablespoons sour cream

1. Move slider to AIR FRY/STOVETOP. Select SEAR/SAUTÉ and set to 3. Select START/STOP to begin cooking. Heat the bacon grease in the pot. Add the onion, celery, and carrots. Sauté for 3-5 minutes until the onions are translucent. Add peas, chicken stock, ham hock, oregano, salt, and pepper. 2. Close the lid and move the slider to PRESSURE. Make sure the pressure release valve is in the SEAL position. The temperature will default to HIGH, which is the correct setting. Set time to 30 minutes. Select START/STOP to begin cooking. 3. When cooking is complete, turn the pressure release valve to the vent position for a quick pressure release. Move slider to the right to unlock the lid, then carefully open it. 4. Ladle into four bowls and garnish each with 1 tablespoon sour cream. Serve warm.

Per Serving: Calories 289; Fat 6.92g; Sodium 1419mg; Carbs 29.53g; Fibre 8.2g; Sugar 9.75g; Protein 29.1g

Creamy Tomato Basil Soup

Prep Time: 15 minutes | Cook Time: 15 minutes | Serves: 4

1 tablespoon olive oil

1 small onion, peeled and diced

1 celery stalk, sliced

8 medium heirloom tomatoes, seeded and quartered

10 g julienned fresh basil

1 teaspoon sea salt

720 ml chicken stock

240 g heavy cream

1 teaspoon ground black pepper

1. Move slider to AIR FRY/STOVETOP. Select SEAR/SAUTÉ and set to 3. Select START/STOP to begin cooking. Heat oil in the pot. Add the onion and celery and sauté for 3-5 minutes until the onions are translucent. Add the tomatoes. Continue to sauté for 3 minutes until tomatoes are tender and start to break down. Add basil, salt, and stock. 2. Close the lid and move the slider to PRESSURE. Make sure the pressure release valve is in the SEAL position. The temperature will default to HIGH, which is the correct setting. Set time to 7 minutes. Select START/STOP to begin cooking. 3. When cooking is complete, turn the pressure release valve to the vent position for a quick pressure release. Move slider to the right to unlock the lid, then carefully open it. 4. Add heavy cream and pepper to the pot, purée the soup with an immersion blender. Ladle into bowls and serve warm.

Per Serving: Calories 199; Fat 15.42g; Sodium 1302mg; Carbs 13.49g; Fibre 3.5g; Sugar 8.92g; Protein 4.32g

Thai Curried Coconut Carrot Soup

Prep Time: 15 minutes | Cook Time: 26 minutes | Serves: 6

1 tablespoon coconut oil

1 small onion, peeled and diced

1 pound carrots, peeled and diced

2 cloves garlic, minced

1 tablespoon Thai red curry paste

960 ml vegetable stock

1 teaspoon honey

240 ml canned coconut milk

1 tablespoon fresh lime juice

¼ teaspoon red pepper flakes

1 teaspoon sea salt

½ teaspoon ground black pepper

10 g julienned fresh basil, plus 3 tablespoons for garnish

1. Move slider to AIR FRY/STOVETOP. Select SEAR/SAUTÉ and set to 3. Select START/STOP to begin cooking. Heat the coconut oil in the pot. Add the onion and carrots. Sauté for 3-5 minutes until onions are translucent. Add the garlic and curry paste. Continue to sauté for 1 minute. Add remaining ingredients, except 3 tablespoons basil. 2. Close the lid and move the slider to PRESSURE. Make sure the pressure release valve is in the SEAL position. The temperature will default to HIGH, which is the correct setting. Set time to 20 minutes. Select START/STOP to begin cooking. 3. When cooking is complete, naturally release the pressure for 10 minutes. Then quick release pressure by turning the pressure release valve to the VENT position. Move slider to AIR FRY/ STOVETOP to unlock the lid, then carefully open it. 4. In the pot, purée soup with an immersion blender, or use a stand blender and purée in batches. 5. Ladle into bowls, garnish each bowl with ½ tablespoon basil, and serve warm.

Per Serving: Calories 151; Fat 5.31g; Sodium 836mg; Carbs 22.65g; Fibre 4.9g; Sugar 9.8g; Protein 5.3g

Cream Mushroom Soup

Prep Time: 15 minutes | Cook Time: 20 minutes | Serves: 6

4 tablespoons salted butter

900 g baby bella mushrooms, sliced

1 tablespoon cooking sherry

1 yellow onion, diced

30 g plain flour

1.4 L mushroom stock (e.g. Mushroom Better Than Bouillon)

or chicken stock

2 teaspoons dried thyme, plus more for garnish

3 cloves garlic, minced or pressed

1 tablespoon seasoned salt

240 ml heavy cream

A few drops truffle oil, to taste (optional)

1. Move slider to AIR FRY/STOVETOP. Select SEAR/SAUTÉ and set to Hi5. Select START/STOP to begin cooking. Melt the butter in the pot. 2. Add the mushrooms, stir well to coat with the butter, and cook, stirring occasionally, for 10 minutes, pausing to add the cooking sherry after 5 minutes. 3. Using a slotted spoon, remove about half of the cooked mushrooms and set aside. 4. Add the onion to the pot with the remaining mushrooms and cook for another 3 minutes, until the onion has softened, and then add the flour and quickly stir to coat everything. 5. Add the stock, thyme, and garlic to the pot, stir to mix well. 6. Close the lid and move the slider to PRESSURE. Make sure the pressure release valve is in the SEAL position. The temperature will default to HIGH, which is the correct setting. Set time to 5 minutes. Select START/STOP to begin cooking. Quick release the pressure when done. 7. With an immersion blender or working in batches with a countertop blender, blend the soup for about 1 minute, until it's a smooth puree. 8. Stir in the seasoned salt, the reserved mushrooms and the heavy cream. 9. Serve topped with any reserved mushrooms, a sprinkle of thyme, and a few drops of truffle oil (if using).

Per Serving: Calories 564; Fat 7.49g; Sodium 1268mg; Carbs 126.83g; Fibre 18.8g; Sugar 7.68g; Protein 18.97g

Chinese Style Bamboo Shoots Soup

Prep Time: 15 minutes | Cook Time: 15 minutes | Serves: 6

1.7 L vegetable stock

60 ml reduced-sodium soy sauce

3 tablespoons rice vinegar

1 tablespoon rapeseed or vegetable oil

1 tablespoon red wine vinegar

2 teaspoons chili-garlic sauce or sriracha

2 teaspoons ground ginger

2 teaspoons seasoned salt

1½ teaspoons sugar

1 teaspoon white pepper

1 teaspoon sesame oil (any kind)

455 g baby bella mushrooms, sliced (or shiitake mushrooms, tough stems removed)

1 can bamboo shoots, drained

1 bunch spring onions, thinly sliced

250 g baby spinach

30 g cornflour

200 – 350 g firm or extra-firm tofu, cut into small cubes (optional)

2 large eggs, whisked (optional)

1. Place all the ingredients in the pot except for the spinach, cornflour, tofu, and eggs. Stir well and top with the spinach. 2. S Close the lid and move the slider to PRESSURE. Make sure the pressure release valve is in the SEAL position. The temperature will default to HIGH, which is the correct setting. Set time to 5 minutes. Select START/STOP to begin cooking. 3. In the meantime, mix the cornflour with 60 ml water to form a slurry. Set aside. 4. When cooking is complete, quick release pressure. Press START/STOP. Move slider to AIR FRY/STOVETOP. Select SEAR/SAUTÉ and set to Hi5. Select START/STOP to begin cooking. 5. Once the liquid begins to bubble, immediately add the cornflour slurry, stir well, and simmer about 2 minutes. 6. Stir in the tofu followed by the eggs (if using). Stir well for about a minute until little egg ribbons form before serving topped with some crispy Chinese noodles, if desired.

Per Serving: Calories 176; Fat 7.36g; Sodium 1226mg; Carbs 21.93g; Fibre 3.6g; Sugar 5.05g; Protein 8.78g

Flank Steak and Pickle Soup

675 g beef flank steak

1.2 L beef or chicken stock

240 ml unsweetened apple cider

3 large dill pickles, quartered lengthwise and sliced into 1 cm pieces

2 tablespoons jarred prepared white horseradish

1 teaspoon dried thyme

¼ teaspoon celery seeds

¼ teaspoon ground cloves

¼ teaspoon ground black pepper

1. Run your hand along the flank steak to determine the grain of the meat. Slice the meat into 1 cm-thick strips against the grain, then cut these strips widthwise into 2.5 cm pieces. Put them and all the remaining ingredients in the pot. 2. Close the lid and move the slider to PRESSURE. Make sure the pressure release valve is in the SEAL position. The temperature will default to HIGH, which is the correct setting. Set time to 22 minutes. Select START/STOP to begin cooking. 3. When cooking is complete, naturally release the pressure for 10 minutes. Then quick release pressure by turning the pressure release valve to the VENT position. Move slider to AIR FRY/ STOVETOP to unlock the lid, then carefully open it. 4. Stir the soup well before serving.

Per Serving: Calories 182; Fat 6.22g; Sodium 880mg; Carbs 4.37g; Fibre 0.7g; Sugar 3.32g; Protein 25.82g

Savoury Ham and Potato Soup

2 L chicken stock

675 g russet potatoes, peeled and diced

675 g deli ham, any coating or fat removed, the meat diced

2 medium celery stalks, thinly sliced

1 small yellow onion, chopped

2 tablespoons butter, cut into small bits

1 teaspoon dried sage

½ teaspoon ground black pepper

240 ml whole or low-fat milk

30 g plain flour

1. Add the stock, potatoes, ham, onion, celery, sage, butter, and pepper to the pot. 2. Close the lid and move the slider to PRESSURE. Make sure the pressure release valve is in the SEAL position. The temperature will default to HIGH, which is the correct setting. Set time to 8 minutes. 3. When cooking is complete, turn the pressure release valve to the vent position for a quick pressure release. Move slider to the right to unlock the lid, then carefully open it. Stir well. 4. Move slider to AIR FRY/STOVETOP. Select SEAR/SAUTÉ and set to 3. Select START/STOP to begin cooking. 5. Bring the soup to a simmer, stirring occasionally, about 5 minutes. Whisk the milk and flour in a medium bowl until smooth. Whisk this slurry into the bubbling soup. Continue cooking, whisking constantly, until thickened, 1 to 2 minutes. Turn off the SEAR/SAUTÉ function. 6. Whisk a few more times to stop the bubbling, then serve hot.

Per Serving: Calories 379; Fat 13.78g; Sodium 1722mg; Carbs 31.1g; Fibre 2g; Sugar 3.03g; Protein 33.82g

Prawns & Noodle Soup

Prep Time: 15 minutes | Cook Time: 11 minutes | Serves: 4

1.5 L vegetable or chicken stock

100 g brown or white rice stick noodles, or rice noodles for pad Thai

80 g shiitake mushroom caps, thinly sliced

2 tablespoons soy sauce, preferably reduced-sodium

1 tablespoon minced peeled fresh ginger

455 g medium prawns, peeled and deveined

200 g small bok choy, washed well for grit and roughly chopped

1. Combine the stock, mushrooms, noodles, soy sauce, and ginger in the pot. 2. Close the lid and move the slider to PRESSURE. Make sure the pressure release valve is in the SEAL position. The temperature will default to HIGH, which is the correct setting. Set time to 4 minutes. Select START/STOP to begin cooking. 3. When cooking is complete, turn the pressure release valve to the vent position for a quick pressure release. Move slider to the right to unlock the lid, then carefully open it. 4. Move slider to AIR FRY/STOVETOP. Select SEAR/SAUTÉ and set to Lo1. Select START/STOP to begin cooking. 5. Bring the soup to a simmer, about 5 minutes. Stir the prawns and bok choy into the soup. Cook, stirring occasionally, until the prawns are pink and firm, about 2 minutes. Turn off the SEAR/SAUTÉ function and serve warm.

Per Serving: Calories 288; Fat 12.62g; Sodium 2122mg; Carbs 7.64g; Fibre 0.3g; Sugar 4.66g; Protein 35.01g

Italian Sausage & White Bean Soup

Prep Time: 15 minutes | Cook Time: 15 minutes | Serves: 6

2 tablespoons olive oil

455 g sweet Italian sausage links, cut into 2.5 cm pieces

4 medium carrots, peeled and chopped

1 medium yellow onion, chopped (

2 medium garlic cloves, peeled and minced (2 teaspoons)

2 teaspoons finely grated orange zest

2 teaspoons dried oregano

Up to ½ teaspoon saffron threads (optional)

½ teaspoon table salt

1.5 L chicken stock

2 large round red tomatoes, stemmed and chopped

One can white beans, drained and rinsed

Up to 2 dried chiles de arbol (optional)

1. Move slider to AIR FRY/STOVETOP. Select SEAR/SAUTÉ and set to 3. Select START/STOP to begin cooking. Heat oil in the pot. Add the sausage pieces. Cook, stirring once in a while, until lightly browned, about 5 minutes. 2. Add the carrots and onion; continue cooking, stirring often, until the onion begins to soften, about 3 minutes. 3. Stir in the garlic, zest, saffron (if using), oregano, and salt until aromatic, just a few seconds. 4. Pour in the stock and scrape up the most of the browned bits on the pot's bottom. Turn off the SEAR/SAUTÉ function and stir in the tomatoes, white beans, and dried chiles (if using). 5. Close the lid and move the slider to PRESSURE. Make sure the pressure release valve is in the SEAL position. The temperature will default to HIGH, which is the correct setting. Set time to 6 minutes. Select START/STOP to begin cooking. 6. When cooking is complete, turn the pressure release valve to the vent position for a quick pressure release. Move slider to the right to unlock the lid, then carefully open it. If you've included the dried chiles, find and discard them. Stir well before serving.

Per Serving: Calories 303; Fat 11.87g; Sodium 1533mg; Carbs 29.18g; Fibre 6.8g; Sugar 5.72g; Protein 21.82g

Spiced Beef & Bok Choy Soup

Prep Time: 15 minutes | Cook Time: 20 minutes | Serves: 6

455 g boneless beef chuck, cut into 2.5 cm pieces

1.5 L beef or chicken stock

60 ml soy sauce

1 medium red onion, chopped

2 medium carrots, thinly sliced

2 tablespoons minced peeled fresh ginger

1 teaspoon five-spice powder

1 large head of bok choy (about 455 g) cored and thinly sliced

1. Add the beef, onion, carrots, stock, soy sauce, ginger, and five-spice powder to the pot. Lock the lid onto the pot. 2. Close the lid and move the slider to PRESSURE. Make sure the pressure release valve is in the SEAL position. The temperature will default to HIGH, which is the correct setting. Set time to 20 minutes. Select START/STOP to begin cooking. 3. When cooking is complete, naturally release the pressure for 30 minutes. Then quick release pressure by turning the pressure release valve to the VENT position. Move slider to AIR FRY/ STOVETOP to unlock the lid, then carefully open it. 4. Stir in the bok choy. Set the lid askew over the top of the pot and set aside for 5 minutes to partially wilt the vegetable. Stir well before serving.

Per Serving: Calories 165; Fat 6.89g; Sodium 1125mg; Carbs 7.5g; Fibre 1.4g; Sugar 4.57g; Protein 19.24g

Delicious Chicken Noodle Soup

Prep Time: 15 minutes | Cook Time: 15 minutes | Serves: 8

1 whole chicken chopped into quarters (leg, breast, thigh, and wing)

1.9 L water

1 Spanish (or yellow) onion, peeled and cut into large chunks

3 cloves garlic, minced or pressed

1 heaping tablespoon Chicken Better Than Bouillon or 4 chicken bouillon cubes

1 teaspoon Italian seasoning

1 teaspoon lemon pepper seasoning

3 bay leaves

Salt and black pepper

200 – 300 g egg noodles

240 g carrots, peeled and sliced into 1 cm disks

240 g celery, sliced into 1 cm pieces with leafy green tops reserved

15 g fresh dill leaves

3 tablespoons fresh parsley, chopped (or 1 tablespoon dried parsley)

2 tablespoons cooking sherry

1½ teaspoons seasoned salt (more to taste)

1. Place the chicken in the pot and pour in water to cover the chicken. Add the onion, garlic, bouillon, lemon pepper seasoning, Italian seasoning, bay leaves, salt and pepper. Stir to mix well. 2. Close the lid and move the slider to PRESSURE. Make sure the pressure release valve is in the SEAL position. The temperature will default to HIGH, which is the correct setting. Set time to 10 minutes. Select START/STOP to begin cooking. 3. In the meantime, cook the egg noodles according to package directions and set aside. 4. When the cooking time of the chicken is up, quick release the pressure. Remove the chicken with tongs and set aside to cool. Remove and discard the bay leaves and onion (if you wish) using a slotted spoon. 5. Add all of the remaining ingredients to the pot except for the chicken and egg noodles, and stir. Close the lid and move the valve to the sealing position. Cook on High Pressure for 5 minutes. Quick release when done. 6. While the pot is cooking the soup, pick the slightly cooled chicken meat from the bones, discarding the bones, skin, and cartilage. Shred the meat and set aside. 7. Stir in the shredded chicken and serve in bowls topped with egg noodles.

Per Serving: Calories 180; Fat 3.86g; Sodium 671mg; Carbs 9.21g; Fibre 1.2g; Sugar 1.24g; Protein 25.93g

Chapter 6 Poultry Recipes

Gingered Chicken with Rice & Mushrooms

Prep Time: 35 minutes | Cook Time: 22 minutes | Serves: 4

5 dried shiitake mushrooms

Boiling water

455 g boneless, skinless chicken thighs, trimmed and cut into 2.5 cm pieces

3 tablespoons oyster sauce

2 tablespoons soy sauce, plus more to serve

2 teaspoons finely grated fresh ginger

2 teaspoons white sugar

Salt and ground black pepper

185 g long-grain white rice, rinsed and drained

2 teaspoons grapeseed or other neutral oil

240 ml low-sodium chicken stock

3 spring onions, cut into 2.5 cm lengths on the diagonal

1. Place the shiitakes in a small heat-safe bowl and cover with boiling water. Soak until softened, about 30 minutes. Remove the shiitakes, reserving 60 ml of the liquid. Remove and discard the stems; thinly slice the caps. 2. Meanwhile, in a medium bowl, mix together the chicken, soy sauce, oyster sauce, sugar, ginger, ½ teaspoon each salt and pepper. Set aside. 3. Stir together the rice and oil in the pot. Stir in the stock, the reserved mushroom liquid and the sliced mushroom caps. Add the chicken and its marinade in an even layer over the top; do not stir. 4. Close the lid and move the slider to PRESSURE. Make sure the pressure release valve is in the SEAL position. The temperature will default to HIGH, which is the correct setting. Set time to 10 minutes. Select START/STOP to begin cooking. 5. When cooking is complete, turn the pressure release valve to the vent position for a quick pressure release. Move slider to the right to unlock the lid, then carefully open it. 6. Move slider to AIR FRY/STOVETOP. Select SEAR/SAUTÉ and set to 3. Select START/STOP to begin cooking. Cook until you hear sizzling, 9 to 12 minutes. Press START/STOP to turn off the pot. 7. Using potholders, carefully remove the insert from the housing. Scatter the spring onions over the rice, cover with a kitchen towel and let stand for 10 minutes. 8. Fluff the mixture, stirring in the spring onions and chicken. Taste and season with additional soy sauce and pepper.

Per Serving: Calories 450; Fat 10.93g; Sodium 816mg; Carbs 70.84g; Fibre 3.3g; Sugar 10.51g; Protein 16.42g

Smoky & Spicy Broiled Chicken Breasts

Prep Time: 15 minutes | Cook Time: 13 minutes | Serves: 4

240 ml water or chicken stock

905 g chicken breasts, skin-on

2 tsp (5 g) smoked paprika

½ tsp cayenne pepper

¼ tsp garlic powder

1 tsp onion powder

¼ tsp coarse salt

¼ tsp freshly ground black pepper

55 g unsalted butter, melted

1. Pour the water or chicken stock into the pot, then add the chicken breasts. 2. Close the lid and move the slider to PRESSURE. Make sure the pressure release valve is in the SEAL position. The temperature will default to HIGH, which is the correct setting. Set time to 8 minutes. Select START/STOP to begin cooking. 3. When cooking is complete, turn the pressure release valve to the vent position for a quick pressure release. Move slider to the right to unlock the lid, then carefully open it. Pour the water out of the pot and transfer the chicken to a plate, set aside. 4. Place the deluxe reversible rack in the pot in the higher broil position. Place the chicken on the rack. 5. Close lid and move slider in the AIR FRY/STOVETOP position. Select BROIL and set time to 5 minutes. Select START/ STOP to begin cooking. 6. Broil until the chicken is browned and crispy. 7. In a small bowl, mix together the paprika, garlic, cayenne, and onion powders, salt and black pepper, then stir in the melted butter. Brush the breasts liberally with the butter mixture and serve immediately.

Per Serving: Calories 485; Fat 29.3g; Sodium 406mg; Carbs 4.4g; Fibre 0.7g; Sugar 0.31g; Protein 48.61g

Creamy Chicken & Peas

Prep Time: 15 minutes | Cook Time: 15 minutes | Serves: 6

4 tablespoons salted butter

455 g baby bella mushrooms, sliced

1 large shallot, diced

1 yellow pepper, diced

1.3 kg boneless, skinless chicken breasts, cut into bite-size pieces

240 ml chicken stock

1 teaspoon garlic powder

1 teaspoon seasoned salt

1 teaspoon black pepper

120 g heavy cream

1 package Boursin spread (any flavour) or 100 g cream cheese, cut into chunky cubes

110 g frozen peas

1 jar roasted red peppers, drained and sliced into 1 cm strips

2 tablespoons cornflour

100 g grated Parmesan cheese

Canned biscuits of your choice, cooked according to package instructions, for serving

1. Place the butter in the pot. Move slider to AIR FRY/STOVETOP. Select SEAR/SAUTÉ and set to Hi5. Select START/STOP to begin cooking. Once the butter's melted, add the mushrooms, shallot, and pepper and sauté for 3 minutes until slightly softened. 2. Add the chicken and sauté for 2–3 minutes, until the chicken is lightly seared and the edges are pinkish-white in colour, but not yet fully cooked. Stir in the chicken stock, garlic powder, seasoned salt, and pepper. Press START/STOP to turn off the SEAR/SAUTÉ function. 3. Close the lid and move the slider to PRESSURE. Make sure the pressure release valve is in the SEAL position. The temperature will default to HIGH, which is the correct setting. Set time to 4 minutes. Select START/STOP to begin cooking. 4. Quick release the pressure when done. Press START/STOP. 5. Mix the cornflour with 2 tablespoons water to form a slurry. Set aside. 6. Stir in the cream, Boursin (or cream cheese), frozen peas, and roasted red peppers and let sit for a minute, stirring occasionally (the residual heat will thaw the peas). 7. Select SEAR/SAUTÉ and set to Hi5. Select START/STOP to begin cooking. Once the sauce is bubbling, immediately stir in the cornflour slurry and Parmesan and let bubble for 30 seconds before turning the pot off by pressing START/STOP again. 8. Serve over biscuits.

Per Serving: Calories 887; Fat 28.67g; Sodium 1621mg; Carbs 122.05g; Fibre 14g; Sugar 17.43g; Protein 44.51g

Sweet & Sour Chicken Legs

Prep Time: 15 minutes | Cook Time: 20 minutes | Serves: 6

240 ml reduced-sodium soy sauce

60 ml unseasoned rice vinegar

12 skin-on chicken legs

50 g granulated white sugar

1. Pour the soy sauce and vinegar into the pot. Then place the bottom layer of the Deluxe Reversible Rack in the lower position in the pot. Pile the chicken legs onto the rack. 2. Close the lid and move the slider to PRESSURE. Make sure the pressure release valve is in the SEAL position. The temperature will default to HIGH, which is the correct setting. Set time to 12 minutes. Select START/STOP to begin cooking. 3. When cooking is complete, turn the pressure release valve to the vent position for a quick pressure release. Move slider to the right to unlock the lid, then carefully open it. Use kitchen tongs to transfer the chicken legs to a large, lipped baking sheet. 4. Remove the rack from the pot. Stir the sugar into the liquids in the pot. 5. Move slider to AIR FRY/STOVETOP. Select SEAR/SAUTÉ and set to 3. Select START/STOP to begin cooking. Allow the liquid to come to a simmer, then simmer for about 3 minutes, or until the liquid slightly thickens. 6. Place the chicken legs in the pot. Stir the chicken in the sauce frequently to coat well, about 5 minutes. Serve warm.

Per Serving: Calories 880; Fat 64.17g; Sodium 932mg; Carbs 12.3g; Fibre 1.1g; Sugar 9.06g; Protein 59.58g

Herbed Chicken

Prep Time: 15 minutes | Cook Time: 36 minutes | Serves: 6

2 tablespoons olive oil

2 tablespoons dried herbs blend

1 teaspoon Salt

One whole chicken, any giblets or neck removed

480 ml chicken stock or water

1. Use a fork to mash or mix the oil, dried herbs, and salt in a small bowl until uniform. Rub this mixture all over the outside of the chicken. 2. Pour the stock or water into the pot. Then place the bottom layer of the Deluxe Reversible Rack in the lower position in the pot. 3. Place chicken on the rack. Close the lid and move the slider to PRESSURE. Make sure the pressure release valve is in the SEAL position. The temperature will default to HIGH, which is the correct setting. Set time to 36 minutes. Select START/STOP to begin cooking. 4. When cooking is complete, turn it off and let its pressure return to normal naturally, about 1 hour. 5. Open the lid. Cool the chicken in the pot for a few minutes, then use large kitchen tongs and a large metal spatula to transfer the bird to a nearby cutting board. 6. Cool for another 5 to 10 minutes, then carve the chicken as desired.

Per Serving: Calories 314; Fat 15.91g; Sodium 804mg; Carbs 2.24g; Fibre 0g; Sugar 0g; Protein 38.02g

Fried Herbed Chicken Thighs

Prep Time: 15 minutes | Cook Time: 35 minutes | Serves: 6

1½ teaspoons mild paprika

1½ teaspoons Salt

1 teaspoon onion powder

½ teaspoon dried sage

½ teaspoon dried thyme

½ teaspoon ground black pepper

¼ teaspoon garlic powder

360 ml water

Six 200 to 250 g bone-in skin-on chicken thighs

Peanut oil, vegetable oil, or solid vegetable shortening, for frying

1. In a large shallow bowl, mix the paprika, salt, sage, thyme, onion powder, pepper, and garlic powder until uniform. Pat the chicken thighs dry with paper towels and roll the chicken in this mixture to coat the pieces evenly on all sides. 2. Pour the water into the pot. Then place the bottom layer of the Deluxe Reversible Rack in the lower position in the pot. Arrange the thighs on the rack. 3. Close the lid and move the slider to PRESSURE. Make sure the pressure release valve is in the SEAL position. The temperature will default to HIGH, which is the correct setting. Set time to 15 minutes. Select START/STOP to begin cooking. 4. When cooking is complete, turn the pressure release valve to the vent position for a quick pressure release. Move slider to the right to unlock the lid, then carefully open it. Line a large lipped baking sheet with paper towels. Use kitchen tongs to transfer the hot thighs to a large, lipped baking sheet. Set aside to dry for at least 20 minutes or up to 1 hour. 5. Clean and dry the pot. Pour in enough oil to come about 1 cm up the bottom. Move slider to AIR FRY/STOVETOP. Select SEAR/SAUTÉ and set to 3. Select START/STOP to begin cooking. Heat until the fat shimmers. 6. Slip three of the thighs skin side down into the oil. Fry until golden and crisp, about 10 minutes. Turn and continue frying until golden, crisp, and cooked through, about another 10 minutes. 7. Transfer the thighs to a wire cooling rack and salt as desired. Add enough oil or shortening to get the depth back to 1 cm if necessary and wait a moment or two make sure the oil is again hot. Fry the remainder of the thighs in the same way. Serve warm.

Per Serving: Calories 208; Fat 21.96g; Sodium 593mg; Carbs 1.29g; Fibre 0.4g; Sugar 0.28g; Protein 2.04g

Honey Glazed Turkey Legs

Prep Time: 15 minutes | Cook Time: 45 minutes | Serves: 4

1 tablespoon standard chile powder

1 teaspoon mild smoked paprika

1 teaspoon onion powder

1 teaspoon table salt

1 teaspoon ground black pepper

2 tablespoons vegetable, corn, or rapeseed oil

Four skin-on turkey legs

480 ml water

60 g honey

1 tablespoon apple cider vinegar

1. Mix the chile powder, smoked paprika, onion powder, salt, and pepper in a small bowl until uniform. Smear ½ tablespoon oil on each turkey leg, then coat them evenly in the spice mixture. 2. Pour the water into the pot. Then place the bottom layer of the Deluxe Reversible Rack in the lower position in the pot. Place the turkey legs on the rack. 3. Close the lid and move the slider to PRESSURE. Make sure the pressure release valve is in the SEAL position. The temperature will default to HIGH, which is the correct setting. Set time to 40 minutes. Select START/STOP to begin cooking. 4. When cooking is complete, naturally release the pressure for 10 minutes. Then quick release pressure by turning the pressure release valve to the VENT position. Move slider to AIR FRY/ STOVETOP to unlock the lid, then carefully open it. 5. Use kitchen tongs to transfer the turkey legs to a plate, set aside. Remove the rack from the pot. 6. Pour out the water from the pot but reserve 2 teaspoons. 7. Move slider to AIR FRY/STOVETOP. Select SEAR/SAUTÉ and set to 3. Select START/STOP to begin cooking. 8. Whisk the honey, vinegar, and 1 to 2 teaspoons of the cooking water in the pot to make a sauce with the consistency of thick barbecue sauce, about 3 minutes. Press START/STOP to turn off the SEAR/SAUTÉ function. 9. Brush some of this honey mixture over the turkey legs. Place the Deluxe Reversible Rack in the pot and place the glazed turkey legs on the rack. Select BROIL. Press START/STOP to begin cooking. 10. Broil the turkey legs to brown and crisp, about 2 minutes, turning a couple of times and basting with more of the mopping sauce. Cool for 5 minutes before serving.

Per Serving: Calories 254; Fat 12.65g; Sodium 649mg; Carbs 19.15g; Fibre 0.7g; Sugar 17.76g; Protein 16.96g

Spiced Chicken Wings

Prep Time: 15 minutes | Cook Time: 10 minutes | Serves: 6

1.5 kg chicken wings, cut into their three parts, any flappers removed and discarded

3 tablespoons dried spice blend

240 ml liquid (Choose from water, beer, white wine, stock,

or unsweetened apple cider)

Up to 1 teaspoon table salt (optional)

200 g coating mixture (such as barbecue sauce, chutney, French dressing, honey mustard, Ranch dressing)

1. In a large bowl, mix together the chicken wing pieces, the dried spice blend, and the salt (if using). Toss well until the chicken pieces are well coated in the spice blend. 2. Pour the liquid into the pot. Then place the Cook & Crisp Basket in the pot. Pile all the coated wings onto the basket. 3. Close the lid and move the slider to PRESSURE. Make sure the pressure release valve is in the SEAL position. The temperature will default to HIGH, which is the correct setting. Set time to 5 minutes. Select START/ STOP to begin cooking. 4. When cooking is complete, naturally release the pressure for 10 minutes. Then quick release pressure by turning the pressure release valve to the VENT position. Move slider to AIR FRY/ STOVETOP to unlock the lid, then carefully open it. 5. Use kitchen tongs or a big spoon to transfer the hot chicken wings to a large bowl. Add the coating mixture and toss well. 6. Turn the coated chicken back to the basket in the pot. Move slider in the AIR FRY/STOVETOP position. Select BROIL and set time to 5 minutes. Select START/ STOP to begin cooking, turning once. Serve warm.

Per Serving: Calories 394; Fat 9.8g; Sodium 1033mg; Carbs 18.69g; Fibre 2.1g; Sugar 8.5g; Protein 55.18g

White Wine Braised Chicken Thighs & Sweet Potatoes

Prep Time: 15 minutes | Cook Time: 35 minutes | Serves: 4

100 g thin strips of bacon, chopped

Four bone-in skinless chicken thighs

1 medium yellow onion, chopped

1 medium green pepper, stemmed, cored, and chopped

1 medium red pepper, stemmed, cored, and chopped

1 teaspoon Dijon mustard

½ teaspoon dried thyme

½ teaspoon caraway seeds

½ teaspoon celery seeds

½ teaspoon table salt

½ teaspoon ground black pepper

120 ml dry white wine, such as Chardonnay; or unsweetened apple cider

120 ml chicken stock

3 medium sweet potatoes, peeled and quartered lengthwise into wedges

1. Move slider to AIR FRY/STOVETOP. Select SEAR/SAUTÉ and set to 3. Select START/STOP to begin cooking. 2. Cook the bacon in the pot until crisp, stirring occasionally, about 4 minutes. Use a slotted spoon to transfer the bacon pieces to a nearby bowl. Add two of the thighs and brown well on both sides, turning a couple of times, about 6 minutes. Transfer these thighs to a bowl, add the other two, and brown them in the same way before transferring them to that bowl. 3. Add the onion and both peppers. Cook, stirring occasionally, until softened, about 4 minutes. Stir in the mustard, thyme, celery seeds, caraway seeds, salt, and pepper until aromatic, just a few seconds. Pour in the wine and scrape up any browned bits on the pot's bottom. 4. Press START/STOP to turn off the SEAR/SAUTÉ function. Pour in the stock and stir well. Return the chicken thighs and any juices in their bowl to the pot. Scatter the sweet potatoes pieces on top of everything. 5. Close the lid and move the slider to PRESSURE. Make sure the pressure release valve is in the SEAL position. The temperature will default to HIGH, which is the correct setting. Set time to 16 minutes. Select START/STOP to begin cooking. 6. When cooking is complete, turn the pressure release valve to the vent position for a quick pressure release. Move slider to the right to unlock the lid, then carefully open it. 7. Use kitchen tongs to transfer the thighs and sweet potato pieces to serving plates or a serving platter. Use a flatware tablespoon to skim any excess surface fat from the sauce. 8. Then, move slider to AIR FRY/STOVETOP. Select SEAR/SAUTÉ and set to Hi5. Select START/STOP to begin cooking. 9. Bring the sauce to a boil and cook, stirring often, until reduced to about half its volume, 2 to 4 minutes. Turn off the SEAR/SAUTÉ function. 10. Spoon this sauce over the chicken and sweet potatoes before serving.

Per Serving: Calories 347; Fat 15.08g; Sodium 1027mg; Carbs 34.88g; Fibre 5.4g; Sugar 12.78g; Protein 20.2g

Lemon Garlic Chicken

Prep Time: 15 minutes | Cook Time: 7 minutes | Serves: 2

120 ml water

2 lemons (zest from 1, juice from both)

2 cloves garlic, crushed

1 tsp dried oregano

455 g boneless, skinless chicken breast

1. Pour the water into the pot. Add the lemon zest and juice, garlic and oregano, then add the chicken to the pot. 2. Close the lid and move the slider to PRESSURE. Make sure the pressure release valve is in the SEAL position. The temperature will default to HIGH, which is the correct setting. Set time to 7 minutes. Select START/STOP to begin cooking. 3. When the timer beeps, quick release the pressure and carefully open the lid. Carefully remove the chicken, slice and serve.

Per Serving: Calories 411; Fat 13.06g; Sodium 608mg; Carbs 52.03g; Fibre 3.8g; Sugar 13.42g; Protein 21.43g

Chicken Artichoke Casserole

Prep Time: 15 minutes | Cook Time: 25 minutes | Serves: 6

900 g boneless, skinless chicken breasts, each breast sliced crosswise into fillets about 1 cm thick

60 g plain flour (seasoned with a pinch each of garlic powder, salt, and pepper)

60 ml extra-virgin olive oil

4 tablespoons salted butter, divided

2 large shallots, diced

3 cloves garlic, minced or pressed

120 ml dry white wine (like a chardonnay)

Juice of 1 lemon

180 ml garlic stock (e.g. Garlic Better Than Bouillon) or chicken stock

2 teaspoons dried oregano, plus more for topping

½ teaspoon Salt

½ teaspoon black pepper

1 tablespoon cornflour

1 can artichoke hearts, drained and quartered

25 g Italian or garlic-and-herb breadcrumbs

25 g grated Parmesan cheese

1. Dredge the chicken on both sides in the flour mixture and set aside. 2. Pour the olive oil and 2 tablespoons of the butter into the pot. 3. Move slider to AIR FRY/STOVETOP. Select SEAR/SAUTÉ and set to Hi5. Select START/STOP to begin cooking. Heat about 3 minutes, until the butter's melted. 4. Working in batches, sear the chicken for 1 minute per side until very lightly browned, remove the chicken with tongs, and set aside on a plate. Leave any excess oil in the pot for more flavour. 5. Add the remaining 2 tablespoons of butter and scrape up any browned bits from the bottom of the pot. Add the shallots and sauté for about 2 minutes, until beginning to brown, then add the garlic and sauté for 1 more minute. Add the wine and lemon juice and bring to a simmer. 6. Add the stock, Salt, oregano, and pepper and stir well, giving the bottom of the pot one last scrape for good measure. Return the chicken to the pot. 7. Close the lid and move the slider to PRESSURE. Make sure the pressure release valve is in the SEAL position. The temperature will default to HIGH, which is the correct setting. Set time to 5 minutes. Select START/STOP to begin cooking. Quick release the pressure when done. 8. Mix the cornflour with 1 tablespoon water to form a slurry. Close the lid and let stand for 10 minutes. 9. Transfer the chicken to a casserole dish that fits the pot. Move slider to AIR FRY/STOVETOP. Select SEAR/SAUTÉ and set to Hi5. Select START/STOP to begin cooking. 10. Once the sauce bubbles, immediately add the cornflour slurry and stir for 30 seconds, as the sauce thickens. Once the bubbles die down, the sauce will have thickened beautifully. Stir in the artichokes and then pour the sauce over the chicken in the casserole dish. 11. Mix the breadcrumbs and Parmesan, sprinkle evenly over the chicken and top with a few more shakes of oregano. 12. Place the deluxe reversible rack in the pot in the higher broil position. Place the casserole on the rack. 13. Close lid and move slider in the AIR FRY/STOVETOP position. Select BROIL and set time to 3 minutes. Select START/ STOP to begin cooking. 14. Remove and serve immediately over rice or angel-hair pasta (cooked separately), if you wish. And of course, get some Italian or French bread to dip in that remarkable sauce.

Per Serving: Calories 487; Fat 21.01g; Sodium 962mg; Carbs 54.84g; Fibre 6g; Sugar 9.39g; Protein 21.7g

Herbed Pomegranate Chicken

Prep Time: 15 minutes | Cook Time: 30 minutes | Serves: 4

2 tbsp (28 g) grass-fed butter, ghee or avocado oil

905 g boneless, skinless chicken thighs, quartered

1 medium yellow onion, thinly sliced

5 cloves garlic, finely chopped

1 tsp sea salt

1 tsp chili powder

¼ tsp ground cloves

¼ tsp ground allspice

¼ tsp ground cinnamon

¼ tsp ground cardamom

60 ml sugar-free 100% pomegranate juice

2 large celery ribs with leaves, thinly sliced

15 g finely chopped fresh flat-leaf parsley, plus more for garnish

1 tbsp (2 g) finely chopped fresh rosemary

1 tbsp (2 g) finely chopped fresh mint

2 tsp (2 g) finely chopped fresh thyme leaves

60 ml honey

1 tbsp (15 ml) quality blackstrap molasses

175 ml chicken or vegetable stock

87 g pomegranate arils, for garnish

1. Place your healthy fat of choice in the pot. Move slider to AIR FRY/STOVETOP. Select SEAR/SAUTÉ and set to 3. Select START/STOP to begin cooking. Once the fat has melted, add the chicken and brown for about 3½ minutes on each side. You may need to do this in two batches if the chicken is too cramped in the pot. Remove the chicken and transfer to a plate. Set aside. 2. Add the onion to the pot and sauté, stirring occasionally, for 5 minutes, or until fragrant. Then, add the garlic, chili powder, salt, cloves, cinnamon, allspice, and cardamom and sauté for 1 minute, stirring occasionally. Add the pomegranate juice and deglaze the pot, scraping up any browned bits with a wooden spoon. Press START/STOP. 3. Add the celery, parsley, thyme, mint, rosemary, honey, molasses, browned chicken and stock, stirring well and making sure the chicken is submerged in the liquid. 4. Close the lid and move the slider to PRESSURE. Make sure the pressure release valve is in the SEAL position. The temperature will default to HIGH, which is the correct setting. Set time to 12 minutes. Select START/STOP to begin cooking. 5. When cooking is complete, naturally release the pressure for 15 minutes. Then quick release pressure by turning the pressure release valve to the VENT position. Move slider to AIR FRY/ STOVETOP to unlock the lid, then carefully open it. 6. With tongs or a large slotted spoon, transfer the chicken to a plate or cutting board. Chop the chicken into bite-size chunks, then set aside. 7. Move slider to AIR FRY/STOVETOP. Select SEAR/ SAUTÉ and set to 3. Select START/STOP to begin cooking. Allow the liquid to come to a simmer, then simmer for about 5 minutes, or until the liquid slightly thickens. Press START/STOP. Add the chicken, give the mixture a stir, taste for seasoning and adjust the salt to taste. Let it rest for 10 minutes. 8. Serve immediately, garnished with fresh pomegranate arils and chopped fresh flat-leaf parsley.

Per Serving: Calories 775; Fat 30.15g; Sodium 1481mg; Carbs 83.34g; Fibre 6.5g; Sugar 41.07g; Protein 43.4g

Gingered Chicken with Almonds

2 tablespoons olive oil

Six bone-in skin-on chicken thighs

1 teaspoon table salt

½ teaspoon ground black pepper

1 large red onion, chopped

2 tablespoons minced peeled fresh ginger

120 g unsalted almonds, chopped

10 g loosely packed fresh coriander leaves

1 tablespoon mild paprika

1 teaspoon ground coriander

300 ml chicken stock

1. Move slider to AIR FRY/STOVETOP. Select SEAR/SAUTÉ and set to 3. Select START/STOP to begin cooking. 2. Warm the oil for 1 or 2 minutes in the pot. Season the chicken pieces with the salt and pepper, then add about half of them skin side down to the pot and brown well without turning, about 4 minutes. Transfer these pieces to a bowl and continue browning the remainder before transferring them to the bowl. 3. Add the onion and cook, stirring occasionally, until softened, about 4 minutes. Stir in the ginger and cook, stirring frequently, for one minute. Stir in the almonds, paprika, coriander, and coriander until fragrant, just a few seconds. 4. Pour in the stock. Press START/STOP to turn off the SEAR/SAUTÉ function. Scrape up any browned bits on the pot's bottom. Return the chicken pieces to the pot, overlapping them so that they mostly fit in the sauce. Pour any juices in their bowl over them. 5. Close the lid and move the slider to PRESSURE. Make sure the pressure release valve is in the SEAL position. The temperature will default to HIGH, which is the correct setting. Set time to 16 minutes. Select START/STOP to begin cooking. 6. When cooking is complete, turn the pressure release valve to the vent position for a quick pressure release. Move slider to the right to unlock the lid, then carefully open it. 7. Transfer the chicken to individual bowls or a large serving bowl. Use a flatware tablespoon to skim any excess surface fat from the sauce. Serve the chicken with lots of the sauce ladled around it.

Per Serving: Calories 398; Fat 33.05g; Sodium 609mg; Carbs 8.88g; Fibre 3.7g; Sugar 2.6g; Protein 19.19g

Delicious Chicken & Sausage Jambalaya

Prep Time: 15 minutes | Cook Time: 17 minutes | Serves: 6

2 tsp (10 ml) extra-virgin olive oil

455 g andouille sausage, cut into 6-mm thick slices

2 boneless, skinless chicken breasts, cut into bite-size pieces

1 yellow onion, chopped

1 red pepper, seeded and chopped

2 celery ribs, chopped

3 cloves garlic, minced

2 tsp (5 g) Cajun or Creole seasoning

½ tsp coarse salt

1 tsp Italian seasoning

475 ml low-sodium chicken stock

300 g uncooked long-grain white rice

1 (411 g) can fire-roasted diced tomatoes, undrained

1. Move slider to AIR FRY/STOVETOP. Select SEAR/SAUTÉ and set to 3. Select START/STOP to begin preheating. Heat the oil in the pot, add the sausage and chicken, cooking until they're browned, about 4 to 5 minutes. Remove the sausage and chicken and set aside. 2. Add the onion, pepper and celery to the pot. Cook until the onion is soft, about 5 minutes, stirring often. Add the garlic, salt, Cajun seasoning and Italian seasoning and cook for an additional 1 minute. Add the chicken stock, stirring well to scrape up any browned bits from the bottom. Press START/STOP to turn off the SEAR/SAUTÉ function. 3. Add the rice, then add the sausage and chicken back to the pot on top of the rice. Pour the fire-roasted tomatoes over all. 4. Close the lid and move the slider to PRESSURE. Make sure the pressure release valve is in the SEAL position. The temperature will default to HIGH, which is the correct setting. Set time to 5 minutes. Select START/STOP to begin cooking. 5. When cooking is complete, turn the pressure release valve to the vent position for a quick pressure release. Move slider to the right to unlock the lid, then carefully open it. Gently stir and serve immediately.

Per Serving: Calories 440; Fat 17.65g; Sodium 1143mg; Carbs 52.9g; Fibre 5.2g; Sugar 3.66g; Protein 20.97g

Flavourful Chicken Vindaloo with Potatoes

Prep Time: 15 minutes | Cook Time: 15 minutes | Serves: 4

2 tbsp (30 ml) avocado oil or extra-virgin olive oil

1 large yellow onion, diced

1 (15-cm) piece fresh ginger, peeled and chopped

6 cloves garlic, minced

1 hot red chili pepper, seeded and chopped

1 (411-g) can diced tomatoes

2 tbsp (32 g) tomato paste

80 ml white wine vinegar

295 ml chicken stock

1 tbsp (6 g) garam masala

2 tsp (4 g) ground coriander

2 tsp (4 g) ground turmeric

1 tsp mustard powder

1 tsp ground cinnamon

1½ tsp (9 g) sea salt, plus more to taste

905 g raw chicken breast, cut into 2.5- to 5-cm pieces

4 medium Yukon gold potatoes, cut into chunks

Cooked rice, for serving (optional)

Chopped fresh coriander, for garnish

1. Move slider to AIR FRY/STOVETOP. Select SEAR/SAUTÉ and set to 3. Select START/STOP to begin preheating. Allow unit to preheat for 5 minutes. After 5 minutes, add oil to the pot, then add the onion, ginger, garlic and chili pepper. Sauté for 3 to 4 minutes, or until fragrant and lightly browned. Select START/STOP. 2. Transfer the onion mixture to a blender. Add the tomatoes, tomato paste, chicken stock, garam masala, coriander, vinegar, mustard powder, turmeric, cinnamon and salt. Blend until smooth, 1 to 2 minutes. 3. Clean the pot to ensure no onion mixture is sticking to the bottom. Return the pot to its base and pour the sauce into the pot. Add the chicken and potatoes. 4. Close the lid and move the slider to PRESSURE. Make sure the pressure release valve is in the SEAL position. The temperature will default to HIGH, which is the correct setting. Set time to 10 minutes. Select START/STOP to begin cooking. 5. Use a quick release, and open the lid once the steam is completely released. 6. Serve plain or over a bed of rice. Season with additional salt to taste and garnish with fresh coriander.

Per Serving: Calories 829; Fat 29.61g; Sodium 1299mg; Carbs 81.43g; Fibre 12.3g; Sugar 10.67g; Protein 59.14g

Chicken Peas Stew with Buttermilk Dumplings

Prep Time: 15 minutes | Cook Time: 32 minutes | Serves: 4

4 tablespoons butter, 2 tablespoons melted and cooled

1 small yellow onion, chopped

2 medium celery stalks, thinly sliced

675 g chicken breast mince

1 teaspoon dried sage

1 teaspoon dried thyme

½ teaspoon ground black pepper

¼ teaspoon celery seeds (optional)

480 ml chicken stock

100 g frozen peas (do not thaw)

2 tablespoons Worcestershire sauce

1 tablespoon Dijon mustard

120 g plain flour

2 teaspoons baking powder

½ teaspoon table salt

120 ml regular buttermilk

½ teaspoon mild paprika

1. Move slider to AIR FRY/STOVETOP. Select SEAR/SAUTÉ and set to 3. Select START/STOP to begin cooking. 2. Melt 2 tablespoons of the butter in the pot. Add the onion and celery; cook, stirring occasionally, until the onion softens, about 3 minutes. Crumble in the chicken and continue cooking, stirring occasionally to break up any clumps, until the meat loses its raw, pink colour, about 3 minutes. 3. Stir in the thyme, sage, black pepper, and celery seeds (if using) until aromatic, just a few seconds. Press START/STOP to turn off the SEAR/SAUTÉ function. Stir in the stock, Worcestershire sauce, peas, and mustard until uniform. 4. Close the lid and move the slider to PRESSURE. Make sure the pressure release valve is in the SEAL position. The temperature will default to HIGH, which is the correct setting. Set time to 5 minutes. Select START/STOP to begin cooking. 5. Meanwhile, whisk the flour, baking powder, and salt in a big bowl. Stir in the buttermilk and 2 tablespoons of melted and cooled butter until a wet dough forms. 6. When the stew has finished cooking, quick release pressure by turning the pressure release valve to the VENT position. Move slider to the right to unlock the lid, then carefully open it. Drop the dough in 6 even blobs across its surface. Sprinkle them with the paprika. 7. Close the lid and move the slider to AIR FRY/STOVETOP, then use the dial to select SLOW COOK. Set the heat to Hi and set the time to 20 minutes. Press START/STOP to begin cooking. 8. When cooking is complete, turn off the SLOW COOK function and open the lid. Set aside to cool for a few minutes, then serve by the big spoonful in bowls.

Per Serving: Calories 624; Fat 24.26g; Sodium 1902mg; Carbs 39.15g; Fibre 2.6g; Sugar 5.06g; Protein 61.5g

Chapter 7 Red Meat Recipes

Homemade BBQ Apricot Pulled Pork

3 tbsp (43 g) grass-fed butter, ghee or avocado oil

1 (905 g to 1.4 kg) pork roast

1 small yellow onion, thinly sliced

5 cloves garlic, chopped

½ tsp chopped fresh thyme leaves

½ tsp chopped fresh rosemary leaves

250 g sugar-free homemade or store-bought barbecue sauce

120 ml cider vinegar

255 g sugar-free all-fruit apricot jam

60 ml pure maple syrup or honey

1 tsp sea salt

1. Place your healthy fat of choice in the pot. Move slider to AIR FRY/STOVETOP. Select SEAR/SAUTÉ and set to 3. Select START/STOP to begin cooking. 2. Once the fat has melted, add the roast and brown for about 3½ minutes on each side. Remove the roast and transfer to a plate. Set aside. 3. Add the onion, garlic, thyme and rosemary to the pot and sauté, stirring occasionally, for 4 minutes, or until fragrant. Add the jam, barbecue sauce, vinegar, your sweetener of choice and salt, giving the mixture a quick stir and scraping up any browned bits with a wooden spoon. Press START/STOP to turn off the SEAR/SAUTÉ function. 4. Place the browned roast in the pot. Close the lid and move the slider to PRESSURE. Make sure the pressure release valve is in the SEAL position. The temperature will default to HIGH, which is the correct setting. Set time to 35 minutes. Select START/STOP to begin cooking. 5. Once the timer beeps, press START/STOP. Allow the unit to release pressure naturally for 15 minutes. Then quick release pressure by turning the pressure release valve to the VENT position. Move slider to AIR FRY/ STOVETOP to unlock the lid, then carefully open it. 6. Carefully remove the roast, place on a large plate or cutting board and pull apart into shreds. Add the shredded pork back to the pot and stir to combine well, ensuring all the pork gets coated. 7. Close the lid and move the slider to PRESSURE. Make sure the pressure release valve is in the SEAL position. Set on high pressure for 5 minutes. 8. Once the timer beeps, press START/STOP and quick release the pressure, carefully open the lid. 9. Stir until everything is fully incorporated. Pour the shredded pork into a shallow dish. Allow the juices to set up and absorb into the meat for 15 minutes. 10. Serve immediately or refrigerate for later use.

Per Serving: Calories 279; Fat 13.7g; Sodium 369mg; Carbs 8.47g; Fibre 0.2g; Sugar 6.41g; Protein 28.57g

Pork Chops with Rice & Vegetables

4 pork chops, thin cut (1cm thick)

1 tbsp olive oil

110 g onions, finely chopped

1 tsp sea salt

1 tsp freshly ground black pepper

185 g basmati rice, rinsed

240 ml water

1 carrot, chopped

70 g mixed vegetables, frozen

1. Pour the oil into the pot. 2. Add the onions at the bottom, then add the rice and sprinkle with salt and pepper. 3. Place the pork on the rice, then pour the water into the pot. 4. Add the carrots and mixed vegetables to the pot. Don't stir. 5. Close the lid and move the slider to PRESSURE. Make sure the pressure release valve is in the SEAL position. The temperature will default to HIGH, which is the correct setting. Set time to 7 minutes. Select START/STOP to begin cooking. 6. When cooking is complete, naturally release the pressure for 10 minutes. Then quick release pressure by turning the pressure release valve to the VENT position. Move slider to AIR FRY/ STOVETOP to unlock the lid, then carefully open it. Serve.

Per Serving: Calories 705; Fat 54.22g; Sodium 682mg; Carbs 19.17g; Fibre 7.3g; Sugar 2.21g; Protein 44.66g

Cheesesteak Mushroom Sloppy Joes

Prep Time: 15 minutes | Cook Time: 20 minutes | Serves: 6

2 tsp (10 ml) olive oil

1 medium onion, sliced

1 green pepper, seeded and sliced

225 g mushrooms, sliced

455 g beef mince

1 (295-ml) can French onion soup

60 ml water

10 ml)Worcestershire sauce

6 buns, split, buttered and toasted

6 slices provolone cheese

1. Move slider to AIR FRY/STOVETOP. Select SEAR/SAUTÉ and set to 3. Select START/STOP to begin preheating. Allow unit to preheat for 5 minutes. After 5 minutes, add the olive oil, then the onion, pepper and mushrooms. Cook, stirring occasionally, until the onion is soft and the mushrooms have released their liquid and it has evaporated, 5 to 7 minutes. 2. Add the beef and cook until almost no pink is left, about 5 minutes. Add the French onion soup and water, ensuring to scrape up any browned bits from the bottom. 3. Close the lid and move the slider to PRESSURE. Make sure the pressure release valve is in the SEAL position. The temperature will default to HIGH, which is the correct setting. Set time to 7 minutes. Select START/STOP to begin cooking. 4. When cooking is complete, turn the pressure release valve to the vent position for a quick pressure release. Move slider to the right to unlock the lid, then carefully open it. 5. Stir in Worcestershire sauce. Divide the meat mixture among the rolls and top each mixture with a slice of provolone

Per Serving: Calories 706; Fat 36.13g; Sodium 707mg; Carbs 64.54g; Fibre 5.5g; Sugar 18.34g; Protein 34.54g

Rosemary-Cherry Pork Tenderloin

Prep Time: 15 minutes | Cook Time: 27 minutes | Serves: 6

1.3 kg pork tenderloin, cut in half

2 tbsp olive oil

½ tsp Salt

½ tsp ground black pepper

120 ml water or vegetable stock

120 ml balsamic vinegar

2 tbsp avocado oil, optional

60 g cherry preserves

4 cloves garlic, minced

10 g fresh rosemary, chopped

1. Move slider to AIR FRY/STOVETOP. Select SEAR/SAUTÉ and sct to 3. Select START/STOP to begin cooking. 2. Heat the oil in the pot. Season the pork with salt and pepper. Add to the pot and cook for 2-3 minutes per side, until browned. 3. In a bowl, combine the water, avocado oil, cherry, balsamic vinegar, garlic, and rosemary, mix well. 4. Pour the mixture into the pot. Press START/STOP to turn off the SEAR/SAUTÉ function. 5. Close the lid and move the slider to PRESSURE. Make sure the pressure release valve is in the SEAL position. The temperature will default to HIGH, which is the correct setting. Set time to 22 minutes. Select START/STOP to begin cooking. 6. When cooking is complete, naturally release the pressure for 15 minutes. Then quick release pressure by turning the pressure release valve to the VENT position. Move slider to AIR FRY/ STOVETOP to unlock the lid, then carefully open it. 7. Remove the pork from the pot. Slice the meat and serve.

Per Serving: Calories 437; Fat 17.37g; Sodium 380mg; Carbs 6g; Fibre 0.4g; Sugar 3.6g; Protein 59.94g

Pork & Chicken Noodles

Prep Time: 15 minutes | Cook Time: 1 hour and 50 minutes | Serves: 2

455 g pork spare ribs, cut into 6 cm pieces
225 g chicken wings
1 tablespoon oil
1 large onion, cut into thick slices
2 garlic cloves, smashed

1 (6 cm) piece peeled fresh ginger
Soy sauce, for seasoning
150 g Japanese ramen noodles, cooked according to package directions

1. Bring 720 ml of water to a boil in a big saucepan on the stove. While the water is boiling, place the ribs and wings inside the pot of the pressure cooker. Move slider to AIR FRY/STOVETOP. Select SEAR/SAUTÉ and set to 3. Select START/STOP to begin cooking. 2. Carefully pour the boiling water into the pot. Allow the meat to simmer for 10 minutes with the lid loosely covering the pot. 3. Press START/STOP to turn off the SEAR/SAUTÉ function. Carefully drain the water from the ribs and wings, transfer them to a large bowl of cold water, and remove any fat. Rinse the cooker pot, dry it thoroughly, and return to the cooker. 4. Select SEAR/SAUTÉ function and set the heat to 3 again. Press START/STOP to begin cooking. Add the oil when the pot is hot. Add the onion and brown for 8 to 10 minutes. Press START/STOP. Add the garlic and ginger, then add the ribs and wings. Fill the pot with water to the ¾ fill line or until everything is submerged. 5. Close the lid and move the slider to PRESSURE. Make sure the pressure release valve is in the SEAL position. The temperature will default to HIGH, which is the correct setting. Set time to 90 minutes. Select START/STOP to begin cooking. 6. When cooking is complete, naturally release the pressure for 20 minutes. Then quick release pressure by turning the pressure release valve to the VENT position. Move slider to AIR FRY/ STOVETOP to unlock the lid, then carefully open it. 7. Using a fine-mesh strainer, strain the stock into a large bowl; reserve the ribs and wings for another use and discard the other solids. Skim any surface oil off the stock, if desired. Season the stock with soy sauce. 8. Divide the ramen between two soup bowls. Pour the stock over the noodles, then serve with the toppings of your choice.

Per Serving: Calories 675; Fat 24.34g; Sodium 425mg; Carbs 32.28g; Fibre 1.4g; Sugar 3.74g; Protein 76.62g

Salsa Verde Pulled Pork with Coriander

Prep Time: 15 minutes | Cook Time: 1 hour and 30 minutes | Serves: 8

220 g mild purchased salsa verde
60 ml liquid from a jar of pickled jalapeño rings
2 tablespoons pickled jalapeño rings

One bone-in pork shoulder or picnic ham, any skin and large bits of fat removed
10 g packed fresh coriander leaves, chopped

1. Mix the salsa verde, liquid from the jalapeño rings, and jalapeños in the pressure cooker pot. Add the pork and toss to coat on all sides. Lock the lid onto the pot. 2. Close the lid and move the slider to PRESSURE. Make sure the pressure release valve is in the SEAL position. The temperature will default to HIGH, which is the correct setting. Set time to 1 hour and 30 minutes. Select START/STOP to begin cooking. 3. When cooking is complete, naturally release the pressure for 30 minutes. Then quick release pressure by turning the pressure release valve to the VENT position. Move slider to AIR FRY/ STOVETOP to unlock the lid, then carefully open it. 4. Use a meat fork and a slotted spoon to transfer the pork pieces to a nearby cutting board. Remove and discard the bone. 5. Use a flatware tablespoon to skim any excess surface fat from the sauce in the pot. Shred the meat with two forks. Add these shreds to the pot along with the coriander. Stir well before serving warm.

Per Serving: Calories 283; Fat 8.64g; Sodium 462mg; Carbs 4.3g; Fibre 1.2g; Sugar 2.14g; Protein 43.82g

Smoked Brisket Skewers

Prep Time: 15 minutes | Cook Time: 53 minutes | Serves: 6

900 g flat- or first-cut lean brisket, cut into 4 cm cubes
1 tablespoon mild smoked paprika
1 teaspoon onion powder
½ teaspoon garlic powder

½ teaspoon table salt
Twelve to sixteen 10 cm bamboo or metal skewers
240 ml water
One bottle liquid smoke

1. Toss the brisket cubes, smoked paprika, garlic powder, onion powder, and salt in a big bowl until the meat is well coated. Thread two cubes onto each of the skewers. 2. Pour the water and liquid smoke into the pot. Then place the bottom layer of the Deluxe Reversible Rack in the lower position in the pot. Pile the skewers onto the rack. 3. Close the lid and move the slider to PRESSURE. Make sure the pressure release valve is in the SEAL position. The temperature will default to HIGH, which is the correct setting. Set time to 50 minutes. Select START/STOP to begin cooking. 4. When cooking is complete, press START/STOP. Naturally release the pressure for 20 minutes. Then quick release pressure by turning the pressure release valve to the VENT position. 5. Move slider to AIR FRY/STOVETOP to BROIL. Set the time to 2-3minutes. Press START/ STOP to begin cooking. 6. Broil the skewers (in batches in the grill pan) until crisp and browned, turning occasionally.
Per Serving: Calories 244; Fat 10.28g; Sodium 447mg; Carbs 1.28g; Fibre 0.5g; Sugar 0.31g; Protein 34.66g

Smoky Corned Beef with Potatoes

Prep Time: 15 minutes | Cook Time: 1 hour and 40 minutes | Serves: 8

1 teaspoon ground dried mustard
1 teaspoon ground coriander
1 teaspoon ground black pepper
One 1.3 – 1.4 kg corned beef, any spice packets removed and discarded, the meat well rinsed

480 ml water
Two bottles liquid smoke
900 g very small, red- or yellow-skinned potatoes, each about the size of a ping-pong balls, scrubbed of any surface dirt

1. In a small bowl, mix together the dried mustard, coriander, and pepper. Dry the corned beef with paper towels, then rub this mixture all over the meat. 2. Pour the water into the pressure cooker pot; stir in the liquid smoke. Then place the Cook & Crisp Basket in the lower position in the pot. 4. Place the coated corned beef on the basket. 3. Close the lid and move the slider to PRESSURE. Make sure the pressure release valve is in the SEAL position. The temperature will default to HIGH, which is the correct setting. Set time to 1 hour 30 minutes. Select START/STOP to begin cooking. 4. When cooking is complete, naturally release the pressure for 40 minutes. Then quick release pressure by turning the pressure release valve to the VENT position, then carefully open it. 5. Transfer the corned beef to a nearby cutting board. Tent with foil to keep warm. 6. Remove the basket from the pot. Stir the potatoes into the liquid inside. Lock the lid. 7. Move slider to PRESSURE. Set to high temperature and set the time to 10 minutes. Select START/STOP to begin cooking. 8. When cooking is complete, naturally release the pressure for 5 minutes. Then quick release pressure by turning the pressure release valve to the VENT position. Move slider to AIR FRY/ STOVETOP to unlock the lid, then carefully open it. 9. Drain the potatoes from the pot into a colander set in the sink. Slice the corned beef against the grain into 1 cm-thick strips and serve with the potatoes.
Per Serving: Calories 269; Fat 18.15g; Sodium 1205mg; Carbs 9.41g; Fibre 0.6g; Sugar 7.6g; Protein 16.88g

Sweet & Sour Beef Short Ribs

Prep Time: 15 minutes | Cook Time: 65 minutes | Serves: 6

1 tablespoon mild smoked paprika

2 teaspoons dried oregano

2 teaspoons dried thyme

1 teaspoon ground dried mustard

1 teaspoon onion powder

½ teaspoon table salt

½ teaspoon ground black pepper

1.3 kg boneless beef short ribs

360 ml water

2 tablespoons vegetable, corn, or rapeseed oil

1 tablespoon granulated white sugar

1 tablespoon apple cider vinegar

1. In a large bowl, mix the smoked paprika, oregano, mustard, thyme, onion powder, salt, and pepper. Add the short ribs and toss they are evenly and thoroughly coated. 2. Pour the water into the pot. Then place the Cook & Crisp Basket in the lower position in the pot. Pile the coated short ribs into the basket. 3. Close the lid and move the slider to PRESSURE. Make sure the pressure release valve is in the SEAL position. The temperature will default to HIGH, which is the correct setting. Set time to 45 minutes. Select START/STOP to begin cooking. 4. When cooking is complete, naturally release the pressure for 20 minutes. Then quick release pressure by turning the pressure release valve to the VENT position. Move slider to AIR FRY/ STOVETOP to unlock the lid, then carefully open it. 5. Use kitchen tongs to transfer the short ribs to a nearby bowl. Pour any liquid in the pot into a second bowl, then clean and dry the pot before returning it to the pressure cooker. 6. Move slider to AIR FRY/STOVETOP. Select SEAR/SAUTÉ and set to 3. Select START/STOP to begin cooking. 7. Warm the rapeseed oil in the pot for a minute or two. Add about a third of short ribs and cook, turning occasionally, until crisped on all sides, about 6 minutes. Transfer these to a serving platter and brown the remaining two batches in the same way. 8. Once all the meat is on the platter, pour the reserved liquid into the pot and bring it to a full simmer. Stir in the sugar and vinegar. 9. Continue cooking, stirring often, until this liquid has reduced to a thick glaze, about 6 minutes. Press START/STOP to turn off the SEAR/SAUTÉ function. Then smear and spread this glaze over the short ribs before serving.

Per Serving: Calories 480; Fat 28.62g; Sodium 443mg; Carbs 3.03g; Fibre 0.7g; Sugar 1.69g; Protein 53.7g

Gingered Honey Beef Short Ribs

Prep Time: 15 minutes | Cook Time: 45 minutes | Serves: 8

12 beef short ribs

2 tbsp olive oil

½ tsp salt

120 ml soy sauce

240 g tomato paste

2 tbsp apple cider vinegar

4 cloves garlic, minced

10 g ginger root, diced

2 tbsp sriracha sauce

60 g raw honey

1. Add oil to the pot. Move slider to AIR FRY/STOVETOP. Select SEAR/SAUTÉ and set to 3. Select START/STOP to begin cooking. 2. Season the ribs with salt. Add to the pot and cook for 5 minutes per side, until browned. Brown the short ribs in batches. 3. Transfer the browned ribs to a plate. 4. Add the soy sauce, apple cider, tomato paste, ginger, garlic, sriracha and honey to the pot. Stir well. 5. Meanwhile, deglaze the pot by scraping the bottom to remove all of the brown bits. 6. Return the ribs to the pot. 7. Press START/STOP to turn off the SEAR/SAUTÉ function. 8. Close the lid and move the slider to PRESSURE. Make sure the pressure release valve is in the SEAL position. The temperature will default to HIGH, which is the correct setting. Set time to 35 minutes. Select START/STOP to begin cooking. 9. When cooking is complete, naturally release the pressure for 10 minutes. Then quick release pressure by turning the pressure release valve to the VENT position. Move slider to AIR FRY/ STOVETOP to unlock the lid, then carefully open it. 10. Serve with the gravy.

Per Serving: Calories 1178; Fat 64.3g; Sodium 1037mg; Carbs 20.3g; Fibre 1.9g; Sugar 16.05g; Protein 132.41g

Braised Chuck Roast with Raisins

Prep Time: 15 minutes | Cook Time: 1 hour and 35 minutes | Serves: 6

1 tablespoon butter

1 tablespoon olive oil

One 1.3 to 1.4 kg boneless beef chuck roast

2 medium yellow onions, halved and sliced into thin half-moons

2 medium garlic cloves, peeled and minced (2 teaspoons)

1 tablespoon stemmed fresh thyme leaves

1 teaspoon fennel seeds

¼ teaspoon grated nutmeg

¼ teaspoon red pepper flakes

1 large round red tomato, chopped

30 g chopped pitted black olives

30 g raisins

300 ml beef or chicken stock

2 tablespoons tomato paste

1. Move slider to AIR FRY/STOVETOP. Select SEAR/SAUTÉ and set to 3. Select START/STOP to begin cooking. 2. Melt the butter in the oil in the pot. Add the chuck roast and brown well on all sides, even around the perimeter, turning occasionally but not too much, about 10 minutes. Use a wide metal spatula and a big cooking spoon to transfer the chuck roast to a nearby cutting board. 3. Add the onions and cook, stirring often, until they begin to soften, about 4 minutes. Stir in the garlic, fennel seeds, nutmeg, thyme, and red pepper flakes until fragrant, just a few seconds. Add the tomato, olives, and raisins. 4. Stir well, turn off the SEAR/SAUTÉ function, pour in the stock, and scrape up any browned bits on the pot's bottom. Whisk the tomato paste into the sauce. Return the beef and any juices on the cutting board to the pot. 5. Close the lid and move the slider to PRESSURE. Make sure the pressure release valve is in the SEAL position. The temperature will default to HIGH, which is the correct setting. Set time to 1 hour 20 minutes. Select START/STOP to begin cooking. 6. When cooking is complete, naturally release the pressure for 30 minutes. Then quick release pressure by turning the pressure release valve to the VENT position. Move slider to AIR FRY/ STOVETOP to unlock the lid, then carefully open it. 7. Use that same large spatula and a big spoon to transfer the roast to a cutting board (the meat may fall into chunks). Cool for a couple of minutes. in the meantime, use a flatware tablespoon to skim the excess surface fat off the sauce in the pot. 8. Chunk the meat into pieces or slice it into 1 cm-thick rounds, then serve in bowls with lots of the sauce.

Per Serving: Calories 269; Fat 14.6g; Sodium 345mg; Carbs 3.88g; Fibre 1.1g; Sugar 1.92g; Protein 31.34g

Pork Chops with Mushroom & Tomato Sauce

Prep Time: 15 minutes | Cook Time: 20 minutes | Serves: 4

4 pork chops, boneless

1 tbsp soy sauce

¼ tsp sesame oil

1 yellow onion, sliced

8 mushrooms, sliced

360 g tomato paste

1. In a large bowl, combine the soy sauce with sesame oil. 2. Add the pork chops and stir until fully coated. Set aside for 15 minutes. 3. Move slider to AIR FRY/STOVETOP. Select SEAR/SAUTÉ and set to 3. Select START/STOP to begin cooking. 4. Put the meat in the pot and cook for 5 minutes oper side, until browned. 5. Add the onion, stir and sauté for another 2 minutes. 6. Add the mushrooms and tomato paste, stir. 7. Press START/STOP to turn off the SEAR/SAUTÉ function. 8. Close the lid and move the slider to PRESSURE. Make sure the pressure release valve is in the SEAL position. The temperature will default to HIGH, which is the correct setting. Set time to 8 minutes. Select START/STOP to begin cooking. 9. When cooking is complete, naturally release the pressure for 10 minutes. Then quick release pressure by turning the pressure release valve to the VENT position. Move slider to AIR FRY/ STOVETOP to unlock the lid, then carefully open it. Serve.

Per Serving: Calories 437; Fat 48.89g; Sodium 207mg; Carbs 22.67g; Fibre 4.7g; Sugar 14.23g; Protein 45.44g

Herbed Lamb And Butternut Squash Stew

Prep Time: 15 minutes | Cook Time: 50 minutes | Serves: 6

2 tablespoons olive oil

1.2 kg boneless leg of lamb, any chunks of fat removed and the meat cut into 5 cm pieces

1 large yellow onion, chopped

2 medium garlic cloves, peeled and minced (2 teaspoons)

240 ml dry white wine, such as Chardonnay

120 ml chicken stock

1 medium butternut squash, peeled, seeded, and cubed

60 g golden raisins

1 tablespoon apple cider vinegar

½ teaspoon table salt

½ teaspoon ground black pepper

1 large rosemary sprig

2 large thyme sprigs

2 bay leaves

1. Move slider to AIR FRY/STOVETOP. Select SEAR/SAUTÉ and set to 3. Select START/STOP to begin cooking. 2. Warm the oil in the pot. Add half the lamb pieces and brown well, turning occasionally, about 8 minutes. Transfer the lamb to a nearby bowl and brown the remaining lamb pieces in the same way before getting them into that bowl. 3. Add the onion and cook, stirring often, until softened, about 4 minutes. Stir in the garlic until aromatic, just a few seconds. Pour in the wine and scrape up any browned bits on the pot's bottom. 4. Press START/STOP to turn off the SEAR/SAUTÉ function and stir in the stock, raisins, butternut squash, vinegar, thyme, rosemary, salt, pepper, and bay leaves. Return the lamb pieces and any juices in their bowl to the pot. Stir well. 5. Close the lid and move the slider to PRESSURE. Make sure the pressure release valve is in the SEAL position. The temperature will default to HIGH, which is the correct setting. Set time to 30 minutes. Select START/STOP to begin cooking. 6. When cooking is complete, naturally release the pressure for 25 minutes. Then quick release pressure by turning the pressure release valve to the VENT position. Move slider to AIR FRY/ STOVETOP to unlock the lid, then carefully open it. 7. Discard the herb sprigs and the bay leaves. Stir well before serving.

Per Serving: Calories 457; Fat 22.26g; Sodium 725mg; Carbs 15.06g; Fibre 1.5g; Sugar 9.79g; Protein 48.23g

Balsamic Garlic Lamb

Prep Time: 15 minutes | Cook Time: 30 minutes | Serves: 6

900 g lamb shanks

1 tbsp olive oil

6 cloves garlic, peeled

240 ml chicken stock

1 tbsp tomato paste

½ tsp thyme

1 tbsp balsamic vinegar

1 tbsp butter

1. Move slider to AIR FRY/STOVETOP. Select SEAR/SAUTÉ and set to 3. Select START/STOP to begin cooking. 2. Heat the oil in the pot. Add the garlic and sauté for 2-3 minutes, or until starting to brown. Pour in the stock and tomato paste. Stir well. 3. Add the thyme and stir. 4. Add the lamb shanks and close the lid. 5. Press START/STOP to turn off the SEAR/SAUTÉ function. 6. Move slider to PRESSURE. Make sure the pressure release valve is in the SEAL position. The temperature will default to HIGH, which is the correct setting. Set time to 25 minutes. Select START/STOP to begin cooking. 7. When cooking is complete, naturally release the pressure for 5 minutes. Then quick release pressure by turning the pressure release valve to the VENT position. Move slider to AIR FRY/ STOVETOP to unlock the lid, then carefully open it. 8. Transfer the lamb to a serving bowl. 9. Add the vinegar and butter to the pot. Stir until butter melts, about 1-2 minutes. 10. Serve the lamb with sauce.

Per Serving: Calories 294; Fat 12.67g; Sodium 307mg; Carbs 2.28g; Fibre 0.2g; Sugar 0.75g; Protein 42.33g

Cheesy Beef and Pasta Casserole

Prep Time: 15 minutes | Cook Time: 20 minutes | Serves: 4

455 g beef mince

2 tbsp butter

1 yellow onion, chopped

1 carrot, chopped

1 celery stalk, chopped

1 tsp Salt

½ tsp ground black pepper

1 tbsp red wine

400 g tomato puree

425 g pasta (of your choice)

Water as needed

150 g mozzarella cheese, shredded

1. Add the butter to the pot. Move slider to AIR FRY/STOVETOP. Select SEAR/SAUTÉ and set to 3. Select START/STOP to begin cooking. 2. Once the butter has melted, add the onion, carrot and celery. Stir until well coated and sauté for 5 minutes. 3. Raise the heat to Hi5. Add the beef mince, ½ teaspoon of salt, and ground pepper. Stir well. Cook, stirring occasionally, for 8-10 minutes until nicely browned. 4. Add red wine, stir well and cook for another one minute, or until the wine has evaporated. Press START/STOP to turn off the SEAR/SAUTÉ function. 5. Add the tomato puree, pasta and ½ teaspoon of salt. Pour enough water into the pot to cover the pasta. Stir well. 6. Close the lid and move the slider to PRESSURE. Make sure the pressure release valve is in the SEAL position. The temperature will default to HIGH, which is the correct setting. Set time to 5 minutes. Select START/STOP to begin cooking. 7. When cooking is complete, turn the pressure release valve to the vent position for a quick pressure release. Move slider to the right to unlock the lid, then carefully open it. 8. Carefully drain off most of the cooking liquid, reserving 120 ml. 9. Add the cheese to the pot, stir and close the lid. Let the dish sit for 10-15 minutes. 10. Serve with the remained sauce.

Per Serving: Calories 561; Fat 21.85g; Sodium 1076mg; Carbs 42.59g; Fibre 8.5g; Sugar 2.69g; Protein 48.67g

Beef & Olives Casserole

Prep Time: 15 minutes | Cook Time: 30 minutes | Serves: 4

455 g stewing steak, cut into cubes

2 tbsp olive oil

2 onions, quarter cut

2 red peppers, quarter cut

1 yellow pepper, cut into thick strips

2 tbsp sun-dried tomato paste

455 g tomatoes, quarter cut

360 ml red wine

125 ml water

50 g black olives

50 g green olives

6 tbsp fresh oregano, chopped

1. Move slider to AIR FRY/STOVETOP. Select SEAR/SAUTÉ and set to 3. Select START/STOP to begin cooking. 2. Heat the oil in the pot. Add the beef and cook, stirring occasionally, for 5 minutes, until browned. 3. Put the onion, red and yellow peppers into the pot. Cook for another 3-4 minutes. 4. Add the tomato paste, red wine, tomatoes, water, black and green olives. Stir well. 5. Press START/STOP to turn off the SEAR/SAUTÉ function. 6. Close the lid and move the slider to PRESSURE. Make sure the pressure release valve is in the SEAL position. The temperature will default to HIGH, which is the correct setting. Set time to 20 minutes. Select START/STOP to begin cooking. 7. When cooking is complete, turn the pressure release valve to the vent position for a quick pressure release. Move slider to the right to unlock the lid, then carefully open it. 8. Top with fresh oregano and serve.

Per Serving: Calories 303; Fat 14g; Sodium 526mg; Carbs 32.92g; Fibre 7.2g; Sugar 13.46g; Protein 11.07g

Egg Salad Sandwiches

Prep Time: 10 minutes | Cook Time: 5 minutes | Serves: 2

6 eggs

30 g chopped celery

2 tablespoons chopped spring onions

60 g mayonnaise

2 tablespoons Dijon mustard

½ teaspoon hot sauce

½ teaspoon Salt

¼ teaspoon freshly ground black pepper

¼ teaspoon paprika

4 slices sandwich bread

1. Add 240 ml to the pressure cooker pot and place the Deluxe Reversible Rack in the bottom. Put the eggs on the rack. 2. Close the lid and cook on high pressure for 5 minutes for hard-boiled eggs. When the timer beeps, naturally release the pressure for 2 to 3 minutes. Then quick release pressure by turning the pressure release valve to the VENT position. Move slider to AIR FRY/ STOVETOP to unlock the lid, then carefully open it. 3. Transfer the eggs to a large bowl and place under cold running water. Peel and chop the eggs as soon as they are cool enough to handle. Transfer to a medium bowl and add the celery and spring onions. 4. In a bowl, combine the mustard, mayonnaise, and hot sauce and mix well. Gently stir the mayo dressing into the egg mixture. Season with the salt, pepper, and paprika. 5. Serve some of the egg salad on the sandwich bread. Store the remaining egg salad in an airtight container in the refrigerator for up to 3 days.

Per Serving: Calories 607; Fat 40.39g; Sodium 1531mg; Carbs 25.83g; Fibre 2.6g; Sugar 4.98g; Protein 33.08g

Cheese Quinoa–Stuffed Pork

Prep Time: 15 minutes | Cook Time: 45 minutes | Serves: 6

1 pork tenderloin

2 tablespoons olive oil, divided

1 clove garlic, peeled and minced

½ medium tomato, diced

10 g chopped fresh flat-leaf parsley

1 tablespoon lemon juice

90 g quinoa, rinsed and drained

480 ml water, divided

30 g crumbled goat cheese

¼ teaspoon salt

1. Butterfly pork tenderloin. Open tenderloin and top with a sheet of plastic wrap. Pound pork out to 1 cm thick. Wrap and refrigerate until ready to use. 2. Move slider to AIR FRY/STOVETOP. Select SEAR/SAUTÉ and set to 3. Select START/STOP to begin cooking. Heat 1 tablespoon oil in the pot. Add garlic and cook for 30 seconds, then add tomato, parsley, and lemon juice. Cook for an additional one minute. Transfer the mixture to a small bowl. Press START/STOP to turn off the SEAR/SAUTÉ function. 3. Add quinoa and 240 ml water to the pot. Close the lid and move the slider to PRESSURE. Make sure the pressure release valve is in the SEAL position. The temperature will default to HIGH, which is the correct setting. Set time to 20 minutes. Select START/STOP to begin cooking. 4. When cooking is complete, naturally release the pressure for 20 minutes. Then quick release pressure by turning the pressure release valve to the VENT position. Move slider to AIR FRY/ STOVETOP to unlock the lid, then carefully open it. 5. Fluff quinoa with a fork. Transfer the quinoa to bowl with tomato mixture and mix well. 6. Spread the quinoa mixture over pork. Top with goat cheese. Season with salt. Roll pork over the filling. Tie pork every 6 cm with butcher's twine to secure. 7. Press SEAR/SAUTÉ and set to 3. Heat remaining 1 tablespoon oil. Brown pork on all sides, about 2 minutes on each side. Press START/STOP to sop cooking. Remove pork and clean out pot. Return to the unit, add remaining 240 ml water, place the Deluxe Reversible Rack in the pot, and place pork on the rack. 8. Close the lid and move the slider to PRESSURE. Make sure the pressure release valve is in the SEAL position. The temperature will default to HIGH, which is the correct setting. Set time to 20 minutes. Select START/STOP to begin cooking. 9. When the timer beeps, quick-release the pressure. Open the lid and transfer the pork to a cutting board. Let rest for 10 minutes, then cut into 2.5 cm slices. Serve hot.

Per Serving: Calories 237; Fat 10.03g; Sodium 177mg; Carbs 10.15g; Fibre 1.3g; Sugar 0.44g; Protein 25.53g

Balsamic Pork Tenderloin with Carrots

Prep Time: 15 minutes | Cook Time: 40 minutes | Serves: 6

900 g pork tenderloin, cut into 2.5 cm pieces
¼ teaspoon salt
¼ teaspoon ground black pepper
2 tablespoons olive oil
1 medium carrot, peeled and sliced
2 cloves garlic, peeled and minced
2 sprigs thyme

1 sprig rosemary
120 ml balsamic vinegar
60 ml water
455 g cipollini onions, peeled
2 tablespoons cornflour
10 g chopped fresh parsley

1. In a medium bowl, toss the pork with salt and pepper until thoroughly coated. Set aside. 2. Move slider to AIR FRY/ STOVETOP. Select SEAR/SAUTÉ and set to 3. Select START/STOP to begin cooking. Heat the oil in the pot. Add carrot and cook until tender, about 5 minutes. Add garlic, thyme, and rosemary, and stir well. 3. Slowly add balsamic vinegar and water, scraping bottom of pot well to release any brown bits. Add cipollini and pork, and stir to combine. Press START/STOP to turn off the SEAR/SAUTÉ function. 4. Close the lid and move the slider to PRESSURE. Make sure the pressure release valve is in the SEAL position. The temperature will default to HIGH, which is the correct setting. Set time to 30 minutes. Select START/STOP to begin cooking. 5. When cooking is complete, turn the pressure release valve to the vent position for a quick pressure release. Move slider to the right to unlock the lid, then carefully open it. 6. Remove 60 ml liquid from pot and whisk in cornflour. Stir mixture back into pot. Press the START/STOP button and set to 4. Bring the sauce to a boil to thicken, about 4 minutes. Press the START/STOP button. Remove pork and sauce. 7. Sprinkle with parsley and serve hot.

Per Serving: Calories 314; Fat 9.93g; Sodium 197mg; Carbs 12.73g; Fibre 1g; Sugar 7.12g; Protein 40.52g

Garlic Pork and Aubergine Casserole

Prep Time: 15 minutes | Cook Time: 20 minutes | Serves: 8

900 g lean pork mince
1 large yellow onion, peeled and diced
1 stalk celery, diced
1 medium green pepper, seeded and diced
2 medium aubergines, cut into 1 cm pieces
4 cloves garlic, peeled and minced
⅛ teaspoon dried thyme
1 tablespoon freeze-dried parsley

3 tablespoons tomato paste
½ teaspoon hot sauce
2 teaspoons Worcestershire sauce
1 teaspoon salt
½ teaspoon ground black pepper
1 large egg, beaten
120 ml low-sodium chicken stock

1. Move slider to AIR FRY/STOVETOP. Select SEAR/SAUTÉ and set to 3. Select START/STOP to begin cooking. Add the pork, celery, onion, and pepper to the pot. Cook until the pork is no longer pink, breaking it apart as it cooks, about 8 minutes. 2. Drain and discard any fat rendered from pork. Stir in the aubergine, garlic, parsley, thyme, tomato paste, Worcestershire sauce, hot sauce, salt, pepper, and egg. Press START/STOP to turn off the SEAR/SAUTÉ function. 3. Pour in chicken stock. Close the lid and move the slider to PRESSURE. Make sure the pressure release valve is in the SEAL position. The temperature will default to HIGH, which is the correct setting. Set time to 10 minutes. Select START/STOP to begin cooking. 4. When the timer beeps, let pressure release naturally, about 25 minutes. Open the lid and serve hot.

Per Serving: Calories 200; Fat 5.52g; Sodium 404mg; Carbs 13.1g; Fibre4.9 g; Sugar 7.02g; Protein 26.67g

Lime Carnitas Tacos with Avocado Crema

Prep Time: 15 minutes | Cook Time: 40 minutes | Serves: 2

For the Carnitas:

455 g boneless pork shoulder roast, cut into 6 cm chunks

Salt

Freshly ground black pepper

240 ml chicken stock

120 ml freshly squeezed orange juice

Juice of 1 lime

110 g sliced onion

2 garlic cloves, crushed

½ teaspoon ground cumin

For the Avocado Crema:

1 medium avocado, halved and pitted, and cubed

15 g coarsely chopped fresh coriander

60 g sour cream

Juice of 1 lime

½ teaspoon Salt

1. Place the pork shoulder meat in the pressure cooker pot. Season with salt and pepper. Add the stock, onion, orange juice, lime juice, garlic, and cumin. Mix well and let the pork marinate for 20 minutes. 2. Close the lid and move the slider to PRESSURE. Make sure the pressure release valve is in the SEAL position. The temperature will default to HIGH, which is the correct setting. Set time to 30 minutes. Select START/STOP to begin cooking. 3. When cooking is complete, naturally release the pressure for 10 minutes. Then quick release pressure by turning the pressure release valve to the VENT position. Press START/STOP. 4. Line a baking sheet with aluminum foil. 5. Transfer the pork to a plate. Carefully strain the juices from the pot through a fine-mesh sieve into a bowl, reserving the cooked onions. Use two forks to shred the meat, discarding any extra fat. Place the pork and onion in a single layer on the prepared baking sheet. 6. Place the Deluxe Reversible Rack in the lower position in the pot. Then place the baking sheet with food on the rack. 7. Move slider to AIR FRY/STOVETOP to BROIL. Set the time to 4-5 minutes. Press START/STOP to begin cooking. 8. Broil until the edges are crispy, then flip the meat, spoon on some of the reserved liquid if necessary, and broil for another 4 to 5 minutes. 9. Scoop the avocado from the skin into the bowl of a food processor fitted with the blade attachment (or into a blender) and add the coriander, sour cream, lime juice, and salt. Process until smooth, stopping to scrape down the side of the bowl with a rubber spatula as needed. 10. Transfer the crema to a small bowl. Cover with plastic wrap and store in the refrigerator for up to 2 hours if not using immediately.

Per Serving: Calories 776; Fat 43.49g; Sodium 1065mg; Carbs 41.26g; Fibre 15.1g; Sugar 11.72g; Protein 60.48g

Balsamic Beef &Vegetable Stew with Olives

Prep Time: 15 minutes | Cook Time: 55 minutes | Serves: 8

455 g beef stew meat, cut into 2.5 cm pieces

2 tablespoons plain flour

¼ teaspoon salt

¼ teaspoon ground black pepper

2 tablespoons olive oil, divided

2 medium carrots, peeled and sliced

2 stalks celery, sliced

1 medium onion, peeled and chopped

200 g whole crimini mushrooms, quartered

3 cloves garlic, peeled and minced

4 sprigs thyme

2 tablespoons chopped fresh oregano

2 bay leaves

60 ml balsamic vinegar

360 ml beef stock

1 can diced tomatoes, drained

1 medium russet potato, cut into 2.5 cm pieces

1 can large black olives, drained and quartered

10 g chopped fresh parsley

1. Add beef, flour, salt, and pepper to a medium bowl. Toss the meat with seasoned flour until thoroughly coated. Set aside. 2. Move slider to AIR FRY/STOVETOP. Select SEAR/SAUTÉ and set to 3. Select START/STOP to begin cooking. Heat 1 tablespoon oil in the pot. Place half of the beef pieces in a single layer, leaving space between each piece to prevent steaming, and brown well on all sides, about 3 minutes per side. Transfer the beef to a bowl and repeat with remaining 1 tablespoon oil and beef. 3. Add the onion, carrots and celery to the pot. Cook until tender, about 8 minutes. Add mushrooms, garlic, oregano, thyme, and bay leaves. Stir well. 4. Slowly add the balsamic vinegar and beef stock, scraping bottom of pot well to release any brown bits. Add tomatoes, potato, and browned beef along with any juices. Press START/STOP to turn off the SEAR/SAUTÉ function. 5. Close the lid and move the slider to PRESSURE. Make sure the pressure release valve is in the SEAL position. The temperature will default to HIGH, which is the correct setting. Set time to 40 minutes. Select START/STOP to begin cooking. 6. When cooking is complete, turn the pressure release valve to the vent position for a quick pressure release. Move slider to the right to unlock the lid, then carefully open it and stir well. Remove and discard thyme and bay leaves. Stir in olives and parsley. Serve immediately.

Per Serving: Calories 209; Fat 7.34g; Sodium 346mg; Carbs 21.77g; Fibre 3g; Sugar 4.14g; Protein 15.61g

Chapter 8 Dessert Recipes

Cinnamon Brown Rice Raisins Pudding

Prep Time: 10 minutes | Cook Time: 25 minutes | Serves: 4

185 g short-grain brown rice
320 ml water
1 tablespoon vanilla extract
1 cinnamon stick

1 tablespoon butter
120 ml raisins
3 tablespoons honey
120 g heavy cream

1. Add rice, water, vanilla, cinnamon stick, and butter to the pot. 2. Close the lid and move the slider to PRESSURE. Make sure the pressure release valve is in the SEAL position. The temperature will default to HIGH, which is the correct setting. Set time to 20 minutes. Select START/STOP to begin cooking. 3. When cooking is complete, naturally release the pressure for 10 minutes. Then quick release pressure by turning the pressure release valve to the VENT position. Move slider to AIR FRY/ STOVETOP to unlock the lid, then carefully open it. 4. Discard the cinnamon stick. Stir in the raisins, honey, and cream. 5. Move slider to AIR FRY/STOVETOP. Select SEAR/SAUTÉ and set to Lo1. Select START/STOP to begin cooking. Simmer unlidded for 5 minutes. Serve warm.

Per Serving: Calories 319; Fat 8.72g; Sodium 32mg; Carbs 55.06g; Fibre 2.5g; Sugar 13.88g; Protein 3.72g

Rice Cream Pudding

Prep Time: 15 minutes | Cook Time: 20 minutes | Serves: 6

185 g basmati rice
300 ml water
480 ml milk
60 g maple syrup

A pinch of salt
1 tsp vanilla extract
180 g heavy cream

1. Rinse the rice well. 2. Add the rice, water, milk, maple syrup, and salt to the pot. Stir well. 3. Close the lid and move the slider to PRESSURE. Make sure the pressure release valve is in the SEAL position. The temperature will default to HIGH, which is the correct setting. Set time to 20 minutes. Select START/STOP to begin cooking. 4. When cooking is complete, naturally release the pressure for 10 minutes. Then quick release pressure by turning the pressure release valve to the VENT position. Move slider to AIR FRY/ STOVETOP to unlock the lid, then carefully open it. 5. Add the vanilla and cream. Mix well. 6. Serve warm with any toppings as you like.

Per Serving: Calories 200; Fat 12.32g; Sodium 161mg; Carbs 22.97g; Fibre 4.1g; Sugar 12.73g; Protein 5.5g

Vanilla Banana Bread

2 large eggs, beaten

100 g sugar

100 g. butter, room temperature

4 medium bananas, mashed

1 tsp vanilla extract

240 g plain flour

1 tsp baking powder

240 ml water

1. In a large bowl, whisk together the eggs, sugar and butter until well combined. Stir in the bananas and vanilla. 2. In a separate bowl, mix the flour and baking powder. 3. Pour the egg mixture into the flour mixture. Stir until the batter is smooth. 4. Grease a baking pan that fits the pot with butter. Pour the batter in the pan. 5. Pour water to the pot and place the Deluxe Reversible Rack in the lower position in the pot. 6. Put the pan on the rack. 7. Close the lid and move the slider to PRESSURE. Make sure the pressure release valve is in the SEAL position. The temperature will default to HIGH, which is the correct setting. Set time to 45 minutes. Select START/STOP to begin cooking. 8. When cooking is complete, naturally release the pressure for 10 minutes. Then quick release pressure by turning the pressure release valve to the VENT position. Move slider to AIR FRY/ STOVETOP to unlock the lid, then carefully open it. 9. Let the bread cool for a few minutes and serve.

Per Serving: Calories 311; Fat 13.13g; Sodium 96mg; Carbs 44.22g; Fibre 2.4g; Sugar 13.65g; Protein 4.67g

Walnuts-Oats Stuffed Apples

30 g chopped walnuts

20 g gluten-free rolled oats

3 teaspoons coconut oil

1 teaspoon maple syrup

1 teaspoon ground cinnamon

⅛ teaspoon salt

4 apples, cored

1. In a small bowl, mix together the walnuts, oats, maple syrup, coconut oil, cinnamon, and salt. Spoon the mixture into the cored apples. 2. Pour 240 ml into the pot and place the bottom layer of the Deluxe Reversible Rack in the lower position in the pot. Place the apples on the rack. 3. S Close the lid and move the slider to PRESSURE. Make sure the pressure release valve is in the SEAL position. The temperature will default to HIGH, which is the correct setting. Set time to 6 minutes. Select START/STOP to begin cooking. 4. When cooking is complete, turn the pressure release valve to the vent position for a quick pressure release. Move slider to the right to unlock the lid, then carefully open it. 5. Serve the apples warm.

Per Serving: Calories 177; Fat 7.37g; Sodium 80mg; Carbs 31.34g; Fibre 6g; Sugar 20.14g; Protein 2.28g

Traditional Peach Cobbler

Prep Time: 15 minutes | Cook Time: 10 minutes | Serves: 6

125 g spelt flour

1 tablespoon baking powder

2 teaspoons coconut sugar

⅛ teaspoon Salt

240 ml buttermilk

900 g frozen sliced peaches

60 ml water

½ teaspoon ground cinnamon

¼ teaspoon ground coriander

1. In a medium bowl, mi together the flour, baking powder, coconut sugar, and salt. Stir in the buttermilk to form a thick dough. 2. Combine the peaches, water, cinnamon, and coriander in the pot. Drop the dough, one tablespoon at a time, on top of the peaches, being careful to not let the dough touch the bottom or sides of the pot. 3. Close the lid and move the slider to PRESSURE. Make sure the pressure release valve is in the SEAL position. The temperature will default to HIGH, which is the correct setting. Set time to 10 minutes. Select START/STOP to begin cooking. 4. When cooking is complete, turn the pressure release valve to the vent position for a quick pressure release. Move slider to the right to unlock the lid, then carefully open it. 5. Let the cobbler cool for 5 to 10 minutes before serving.

Per Serving: Calories 263; Fat 1.27g; Sodium 143mg; Carbs 60.75g; Fibre 6g; Sugar 38.29g; Protein 6.54g

Cinnamon Apples with Dates

Prep Time: 15 minutes | Cook Time: 3 minutes | Serves: 6

4 large Granny Smith or Pink Lady apples, peeled, cored, and sliced

120 ml water

30 g chopped pitted dates

1 teaspoon ground cinnamon

¼ teaspoon vanilla extract

1 teaspoon unsalted butter

1. Place the apples, dates, water, and cinnamon in the pot. Close the lid and move the slider to PRESSURE. Make sure the pressure release valve is in the SEAL position. The temperature will default to HIGH, which is the correct setting. Set time to 3 minutes. Select START/STOP to begin cooking. 2. When the timer beeps, quick-release the pressure. Open the lid. Stir in vanilla and butter. Serve hot or chilled.

Per Serving: Calories 114; Fat 1.05g; Sodium 5mg; Carbs 27.88g; Fibre 3.4g; Sugar 24.1g; Protein 0.44g

Red Wine Braised Pears

480 ml water

480 ml red wine

60 g honey

4 whole cloves

2 cinnamon sticks

1 star anise

1 teaspoon vanilla bean paste

4 Bartlett pears, peeled

1. Place all ingredients in the pot. Stir to combine. Close the lid and move the slider to PRESSURE. Make sure the pressure release valve is in the SEAL position. The temperature will default to HIGH, which is the correct setting. Set time to 3 minutes. Select START/STOP to begin cooking. 2. When cooking is complete, turn the pressure release valve to the vent position for a quick pressure release. Move slider to the right to unlock the lid, then carefully open it. With a slotted spoon, remove pears to a plate and let cool for 5 minutes. Serve warm.

Per Serving: Calories 206; Fat 0.89g; Sodium 19mg; Carbs 50.49g; Fibre 8g; Sugar 36.54g; Protein 2.06g

Sweet Cranberry Applesauce

130 g whole cranberries

4 medium tart apples, peeled, cored, and grated

4 medium sweet apples, peeled, cored, and grated

1½ tablespoons grated orange zest

60 ml orange juice

60 g dark brown sugar

50 g granulated sugar

1 tablespoon unsalted butter

2 teaspoons ground cinnamon

½ teaspoon ground cloves

¼ teaspoon ground black pepper

⅛ teaspoon salt

1 tablespoon lemon juice

1. Place all ingredients in the pot and stir well. 2. Close the lid and move the slider to PRESSURE. Make sure the pressure release valve is in the SEAL position. The temperature will default to HIGH, which is the correct setting. Set time to 5 minutes. Select START/STOP to begin cooking. 3. When cooking is complete, naturally release the pressure for 25 minutes. Then quick release pressure by turning the pressure release valve to the VENT position. Move slider to AIR FRY/ STOVETOP to unlock the lid, then carefully open it. 4. Lightly mash fruit with a fork. Stir well. Serve warm or cold.

Per Serving: Calories 153; Fat 1.35g; Sodium 43mg; Carbs 37.76g; Fibre 4.8g; Sugar 29.8g; Protein 0.67g

Lemon Blueberry Compote

Prep Time: 10 minutes | Cook Time: 5 minutes | Serves: 8

1 (400 g) bag frozen blueberries, thawed

50 g sugar

1 tablespoon lemon juice

2 tablespoons cornflour

2 tablespoons water

¼ teaspoon vanilla extract

¼ teaspoon grated lemon zest

1. Add the blueberries, lemon juice and sugar to the pot. Close the lid and move the slider to PRESSURE. Make sure the pressure release valve is in the SEAL position. The temperature will default to HIGH, which is the correct setting. Set time to 1 minute. Select START/STOP to begin cooking. 2. When cooking is complete, press START/STOP and quick release pressure by turning the pressure release valve to the VENT position. Move slider to the right to unlock the lid, then carefully open it. 3. Move slider to AIR FRY/STOVETOP. Select SEAR/SAUTÉ and set to Lo1. Select START/STOP to begin cooking. In a bowl, combine cornflour and water. Stir into blueberry mixture and cook until mixture comes to a boil and thickens, about 3 to 4 minutes. Press the START/STOP button and stir in vanilla and lemon zest. Serve right away or refrigerate until ready to serve.

Per Serving: Calories 599; Fat 7.26g; Sodium 12mg; Carbs 143.11g; Fibre 30.6g; Sugar 38.95g; Protein 4.78g

Apple Cake

Prep Time: 15 minutes | Cook Time: 55 minutes | Serves: 6

2 tablespoons ground flaxseed

5 tablespoons water, plus 360 ml

3 medium apples, peeled, cored, and diced

3 teaspoons apple pie spice, divided

1 tablespoon maple syrup, plus 80 g

125 g gluten-free flour blend

115 g gluten-free oat flour

2 teaspoons baking powder

½ teaspoon salt

240 g simple applesauce or no-sugar-added store-bought

1 teaspoon pure vanilla extract

Nonstick cooking spray

1. In a small bowl, mix together the flaxseed and the 5 tablespoons of water. Set aside. 2. In a medium bowl, toss the apples with 2 teaspoons of the apple pie spice and 1 tablespoon of the maple syrup. In a large bowl, whisk together the flour blend, oat flour, salt, baking powder, and the remaining 1 teaspoon of apple pie spice. 3. In a medium bowl, combine the applesauce, flax mixture, vanilla, and the remaining maple syrup, stir to mix well. Pour the wet ingredients into the dry and mix well. 4. Spray a cake pan that fits the pot with nonstick cooking spray. Pour and spread half the batter into the pan. Top with half the apples. Repeat with the remaining batter and apples. Cover tightly with aluminum foil. 5. Pour the remaining 360 ml of water into the pot and place the Deluxe Reversible Rack in the lower position in the pot. Place the cake pan on the rack. 6. Close the lid and move the slider to PRESSURE. Make sure the pressure release valve is in the SEAL position. The temperature will default to HIGH, which is the correct setting. Set time to 55 minutes. Select START/STOP to begin cooking. 7. When the cook time is complete, let the pressure release naturally and carefully open the lid. Cool for 5 minutes before turning out onto a cooling rack to cool completely.

Per Serving: Calories 315; Fat 3.52g; Sodium 243mg; Carbs 70.32g; Fibre 5g; Sugar 45.55g; Protein 3.94g

Delicious Chocolate Rice Pudding

Prep Time: 15 minutes | Cook Time: 20 minutes | Serves: 6

480 ml almond milk

185 g long-grain brown rice

2 tablespoons Dutch-processed cocoa powder

60 g maple syrup

1 teaspoon vanilla extract

55 g chopped dark chocolate

1. Combine the almond milk, rice, maple syrup, cocoa, and vanilla in the pot. Stir well. 2. Close the lid and move the slider to PRESSURE. Make sure the pressure release valve is in the SEAL position. The temperature will default to HIGH, which is the correct setting. Set time to 20 minutes. Select START/STOP to begin cooking. 3. When the timer beeps, let pressure release naturally for 15 minutes, then quick release the remaining pressure. Press the START/STOP button and open lid. Serve warm, sprinkled with chocolate.

Per Serving: Calories 317; Fat 11.86g; Sodium 43mg; Carbs 46.32g; Fibre 3.7g; Sugar 16.96g; Protein 6.81g

Lemon Pecans Cake with Chickpeas Filling

Prep Time: 20 minutes | Cook Time: 25 minutes | Serves: 8

4 pitted dates

180 g walnuts

240 g raw cashews, soaked in boiling water for 20 minutes

210 g cooked chickpeas, drained and rinsed

70 g maple syrup

2 tablespoons tahini

2 tablespoons apple cider vinegar

Zest and juice of 2 lemons

1 can full-fat coconut milk

2 tablespoons arrowroot powder

½ teaspoon salt (optional)

360 ml water

Lemon slices, for garnish

1. Cover the dates with hot water and soak for 10 minutes. Drain, reserving the soaking water, roughly chop the dates. Add them to a food processor with the walnuts. Blend until sticky, adding a few drops of the reserved soaking liquid as needed. Press firmly into the bottom of a nonstick springform pan that fits the pot. Set aside. 2. In a food processor, combine the cashews, chickpeas, tahini, vinegar, maple syrup, and lemon zest and juice. Blend until smooth. Add the milk, arrowroot, and salt (if using). Blend to combine. 3. Pour the filling into the crust. Cover the pan tightly with aluminum foil. Pour the water into the pot and place the bottom layer of the Deluxe Reversible Rack in the lower position in the pot. Place the pan on the rack. 4. Close the lid and move the slider to PRESSURE. Make sure the pressure release valve is in the SEAL position. The temperature will default to HIGH, which is the correct setting. Set time to 25 minutes. Select START/STOP to begin cooking. 5. When cooking is complete, turn the pressure release valve to the vent position for a quick pressure release. Move slider to the right to unlock the lid, then carefully open it. 6. Remove the pan, then the foil, and cool for 30 minutes before turning out onto a serving platter. Garnish with lemon slices. Chill at least 6 hours before serving.

Per Serving: Calories 540; Fat 40.34g; Sodium 168mg; Carbs 41.37g; Fibre 5.5g; Sugar 19.42g; Protein 11.31g

Banana Pecans Pudding Cake

Prep Time: 15 minutes | Cook Time: 20 minutes | Serves: 6

3 tablespoons ground golden flaxseed meal

10 tablespoons water, divided

3 mashed bananas

60 ml avocado oil

1 teaspoon pure vanilla extract

250 g almond flour

50 g erythritol

1 teaspoon baking powder

¼ teaspoon salt

65 g chopped pecans

½ teaspoon ground cinnamon

1. Combine the flaxseed and 9 tablespoons water in a small bowl and give it time to gel. 2. In a big bowl, whisk together the flaxseed and water mixture, oil, banana, and vanilla. 3. Stir in the flour, baking powder, erythritol, and salt. 4. Spray a cake pan that fits the pot with nonstick cooking spray. Pour the batter into the pan. 5. In a bowl, mix the chopped pecans, cinnamon, and 1 tablespoon water. Sprinkle on top of the cake batter. 6. Pour 240 ml water into the inner pot and place the Deluxe Reversible Rack in the lower position in the pot. Place the pan on top of the rack. 7. Close the lid and move the slider to PRESSURE. Make sure the pressure release valve is in the SEAL position. The temperature will default to HIGH, which is the correct setting. Set time to 20 minutes. Select START/STOP to begin cooking. 8. When cooking is complete, turn the pressure release valve to the vent position for a quick pressure release. Move slider to the right to unlock the lid, then carefully open it. 9. Spoon into six bowls and serve.

Per Serving: Calories 304; Fat 17.93g; Sodium 101mg; Carbs 37.43g; Fibre 5.3g; Sugar 22.46g; Protein 2.93g

Tasty Coconut Cake

Prep Time: 15 minutes | Cook Time: 40 minutes | Serves: 4

110 g almond flour

50 g unsweetened shredded coconut

45 g erythritol

1 teaspoon baking powder

1 teaspoon ground cinnamon

½ teaspoon ground ginger

2 large eggs lightly whisked

60 ml coconut oil, melted

120 ml unsweetened full-fat canned coconut milk

1. In a large bowl, whisk together the flour, coconut, baking powder, erythritol, cinnamon, and ginger. Whisk in the eggs, coconut oil, and coconut milk and stir until well combined. 2. Spray a 15 cm springform pan with nonstick cooking spray. Pour the cake batter into the pan. 3. Add 480 ml water to the pot and place the Deluxe Reversible Rack inside. Place the pan on top of the rack. 4. Close the lid and move the slider to PRESSURE. Make sure the pressure release valve is in the SEAL position. The temperature will default to HIGH, which is the correct setting. Set time to 40 minutes. Select START/STOP to begin cooking. 5. When cooking is complete, naturally release the pressure for 10 minutes. Then quick release pressure by turning the pressure release valve to the VENT position. Move slider to AIR FRY/ STOVETOP to unlock the lid, then carefully open it. 6. Allow the cake to cool for 5-10 minutes before slicing to serve.

Per Serving: Calories 287; Fat 25.19g; Sodium 195mg; Carbs 13.22g; Fibre 1.4g; Sugar 10.66g; Protein 4.78g

Apple Crisp with Pecans-Oats Topping

Prep Time: 15 minutes | Cook Time: 17 minutes | Serves: 4

For the Filling:

4 large apples, peeled, cored, and cut into wedges

2 tablespoons lemon juice

50 g erythritol

For the Topping:

110 g almond flour

40 g erythritol

80 g old fashioned rolled oats

60 g chopped pecans

¼ teaspoon ground cinnamon

1 teaspoon pure vanilla extract

2 tablespoons almond flour

¾ teaspoon ground cinnamon

1½ teaspoons vanilla extract

60 ml coconut oil

2 tablespoons water

1. To make the Filling: In a medium bowl, mix together the filling ingredients: apples, lemon juice, erythritol, vanilla, cinnamon, and almond flour. Transfer to a 15 cm cake pan and set aside. 2. To make the Topping: In a big bowl, combine the topping ingredients: almond flour, erythritol, pecans, oats, vanilla extract, cinnamon, oil, and water. Use your hands to incorporate the coconut oil into the rest of the ingredients evenly. 3. Pour the topping over the apple filling. 4. Pour 480 ml water into the pot and place the Deluxe Reversible Rack inside. Place the pan on the rack. 5. Close the lid and move the slider to PRESSURE. Make sure the pressure release valve is in the SEAL position. The temperature will default to HIGH, which is the correct setting. Set time to 17 minutes. Select START/STOP to begin cooking. 6. When cooking is complete, turn the pressure release valve to the vent position for a quick pressure release. Move slider to the right to unlock the lid, then carefully open it. 7. Spoon into four bowls and serve.

Per Serving: Calories 449; Fat 25.04g; Sodium 4mg; Carbs 64.14g; Fibre 10.7g; Sugar 38.76g; Protein 6.03g

Cinnamon Dried Fruit Compote

Prep Time: 15 minutes | Cook Time: 9 minutes | Serves: 6

200 g dried apricots, quartered

200 g dried peaches, quartered

120 g golden raisins

360 ml orange juice

1 cinnamon stick

4 whole cloves

1. Place all ingredients in the pot. Stir to combine. Close the lid and move the slider to PRESSURE. Make sure the pressure release valve is in the SEAL position. The temperature will default to HIGH, which is the correct setting. Set time to 3 minutes. Select START/STOP to begin cooking. 2. When the timer beeps, let pressure release naturally, about 20 minutes. Press the START/STOP button and open lid. 3. Discard the cinnamon stick and cloves. Press the SEAR/SAUTÉ button and set to Lo1, simmer for 5–6 minutes. Serve warm or allow to cool, and then cover and refrigerate for up to a week.

Per Serving: Calories 178; Fat 0.46g; Sodium 12mg; Carbs 45.97g; Fibre 3.1g; Sugar 36.05g; Protein 1.83g

Conclusion

A Most people are familiar with the Ninja Kitchen System, but the Ninja Foodi MAX Multi-Cooker is a bit different. The Multi-Cooker is a countertop appliance that can slow cook, steam, and sear/sauté. The Ninja MAX Multi-Cooker is a great addition to any kitchen, and it's especially handy if you have limited counter space. It's easy to use, and the built-in strainer is a major time saver. If you're looking for a versatile appliance that can do it all, the Ninja MAX Multi-Cooker is a perfect choice.

Appendix Recipes Index

Homemade BBQ Apricot Pulled Pork71

Honey Glazed Turkey Legs 63

I

Italian Sausage & White Bean Soup57

Italian Sausage and Rocket Risotto 24

J

Juicy Pulled Pork Sliders 34

L

Lemon Blueberry Compote 88

Lemon Garlic Chicken 64

Lemon Pecans Cake with Chickpeas Filling 89

Lemon-Garlic Smashed Red Potatoes42

Lentils Burger Salad with Special Sauce27

Lime Carnitas Tacos with Avocado Crema 81

Lime Cauliflower Rice with Coriander45

M

Maple Quinoa, Blueberry & Yogurt Breakfast Bowls 19

Maple Steel-Cut Oatmeal with Fruit18

Mushroom, Peas & Barley "Risotto"30

O

Orange Banana Oatmeal Muffins 22

P

Parmesan Crab and Courgette Dip 36

Pecans & Marshmallows Loaded Sweet Potatoes 45

Pickle Deviled Eggs 37

Pork & Chicken Noodles 73

Pork Chops with Mushroom & Tomato Sauce 76

Pork Chops with Rice & Vegetables 71

Potato Yogurt Salad 44

Prawns & Noodle Soup 57

Prawns with Thai-Style Sauce 36

R

Raspberry Breakfast Cake 16

Raspberry Steel Cut Oats Bars 21

Red Wine Braised Mushroom 43

Red Wine Braised Pears 87

Rice Cream Pudding 84

Rosemary-Cherry Pork Tenderloin 72

S

Salsa Verde Pulled Pork with Coriander 73

Savoury Beef and Lentil Soup 52

Savoury Ham and Potato Soup 56

Savoy Beef Stuffed Cabbage Rolls 39

Simple Garlic Chickpeas 25

Smoked Brisket Skewers 74

Smoky & Spicy Broiled Chicken Breasts 60

Smoky Corned Beef with Potatoes 74

Sour Cream Cabbage 41

Sour Cream Deviled Eggs with Olives35

Spiced Beef & Bok Choy Soup 58

Spiced Chicken Wings 63

Spicy Creamy Black Beans 28

Spicy Dill Deviled Eggs 33

Sweet & Sour Beef Short Ribs 75

Sweet & Sour Chicken Legs 61

Sweet Cranberry Applesauce 87

T

Taco Beans Salad 31

Tasty Coconut Cake 90

Tasty Sweet Potato Risotto 31

Thai Curried Coconut Carrot Soup 54

Thyme Beef Stock 51

Thyme Celery Root–Cauliflower Mash with Caramelized Onion 42

Toast with Sweet & Spicy Tomato Jam15

Tomato and Beans Soup 53

Traditional Peach Cobbler 86

Traditional Shakshuka 13

Turkey Cabbage Dumplings 35

Turkey Celery Stock 51

V

Vanilla Banana Bread 85

Vegetarian Red Kidney Beans & Brown Rice 29

W

Walnuts-Oats Stuffed Apples 85

White Wine Braised Chicken Thighs & Sweet Potatoes 64

Wild Blueberry and Quinoa Porridge21

Wild Rice with Hazelnuts & Apricots30

Printed in Great Britain
by Amazon

57828650R00056